Shop 8 m

159

RUN-AND-SHOOT FOOTBALL:
The Now Attack

Glenn "Tiger" Ellison

PARKER PUBLISHING COMPANY, INC.
WEST NYACK, NEW YORK

© 1984, 1965 *by*

Parker Publishing Company, Inc.

West Nyack, New York

10   9   8   7   6   5

Library of Congress Cataloging in Publication Data

Ellison, Glenn.
  Run-and-shoot football.

  Includes index.
    1. Football--Offense.   2. Football--Coaching.
I. Title.
GV951.8.E45   796.332′2   84-14786
ISBN 0-13-783879-4

ISBN 0-13-783879-4

Printed in the United States of America

Dedication

To El Nibaca whose very presence makes life a joy to live, and to Mom and Pop who gave me that life to enjoy.

Foreword

I lured "Tiger" Ellison away from Middletown, Ohio, where he was firmly fixed in a coaching position he often said he would never leave. He was totally dedicated to the town and to its high school, most especially to its football program. I got him in ten short minutes with one long word: dedication.

"Ellison," I said, "you're the forward-passingest coach in the country, and they say I'm the most non-passing coach that ever lived. Yet I want you at Ohio State because of one thing you possess: dedication—to your family and to your school and to your community and to the great game of American football."

In his book Ellison goes further toward opening up the game than any other coach I have known. His daring departure from traditional football will amaze you. But I have seen his teams play. I have studied their movies. His fantastic offense had fantastic success. It is a crowd pleaser. You could almost bet every year that his quarterback would make the all-state team. Yet those quarterbacks seemingly possessed only average physical ability. I suspect that their success can be wrapped up in one word: dedication—to their coach and to their cause.

I am sure that every coach, regardless of the level on which he works, will profit from a study of the revolutionary ideas expressed in this book.

W. W. Hayes
Former Head Football Coach
Ohio State University

Introduction

Following the publication of *Run and Shoot Football: Offense of the Future* in 1965, a deluge of letters and post cards came pouring into my office. Day after day they came—from every state in the Union . . . a few from Canada . . . even one from Germany.

Why all this furor over a coaching book? Because here was the exciting story of the most revolutionary offense in the history of American football. A revolt that started in the mind of a harassed coach ended in a new order of things on the football field. The revolution awakened a sleepy community into wide-eyed enthusiasm and caused that veteran coach, squirming with frustration on the threshold of his first losing season, to wake up and enjoy life to the fullest. In the wake of that revolution came an explosion of touchdowns popping at the rate of one touchdown every ten plays or five touchdowns per game for the next four years, prompting Woody Hayes to invite that high school coach to come to work at Ohio State University. I was that coach.

Why did I desert my faithful old grunt-and-grind offense of twenty-five years for such a wide-open extravaganza as the LONESOME POLECAT?

Coach, I had to do it—I was in trouble. After five games we were suffering from four defeats and one scoreless tie. Our young men were slinking around school with their heads hanging low. On game nights I could feel the vibrations flashing from the stands:

"Hey, Coach. Shape up or ship out!"

Something drastic had to be done . . . but what? Then one day I stopped my car alongside a vacant lot to watch a group of exuberant grade-schoolers toss a football around. They were playing a game they called aerial. The passer was a slender, willowy young man with a rubbery arm. He would scramble around big-eyed and expectant as he studied his receivers cutting downfield right or left or deep or short—according to how the defenders were covering them.

Those youngsters were simply doing what comes natural, letting the defense determine their pass cuts:

He right, I left!
He left, I right!
He come, I go!
He go, I stay!

Boom! There it was: THE LONESOME POLECAT! I went to school the next morning with the craziest idea for scoring touchdowns ever known to man. My coaches thought the rigors of a losing season had caused their head man to slip over the hump.

"This is absolutely crazy!" cried my line coach, Stan Lewis.

Some of my best friends scoffed and said I didn't know what I was doing. Maybe I didn't. But neither did our opponents. The crazy offense worked—oh, how it worked!

Our fans, who had begun staying home on game nights and playing bridge, came flocking back to the stadium. And the LONESOME POLECAT turned a losing season into a winner.

During this turnaround we learned two important lessons:

1. An average passer with average receivers can move the football if they all follow a few simple rules.

2. Average players can become better-than-average passers and receivers if they master a few basic fundamentals.

The success of the LONESOME POLECAT encouraged us the next year to develop a system of advancing the football that we called the RUN AND SHOOT, stealing a term from the basketball people.

The new offense featured running as well as passing and proved to be absolutely sensational. Nobody could stop it. We couldn't stop it ourselves. One night we scored 98 points against Portsmouth, Ohio, a long-time rival. We didn't mean to humiliate those people. But we couldn't turn the thing off. When the embarrassing fiasco was over, our third-string quarterback was top scorer in the Greater-Ohio League. Amazing!

Following the publication of the original *Run and Shoot* book, high schools, colleges, and even some of the pros began to make use of the offense in part or in totality.

What a thrill it was to watch the incomparable Dan Fouts, though a strict drop-back passer, team up with his receivers in executing the San Diego pass offense according to LONESOME POLECAT pass-cut principles.

How exhilarating to watch Coach "Mouse" Davis's Portland State team inundate opponents by flooding the environment with RUN AND SHOOT passes.

And speaking of thrills, do you remember the day Coach Charley Pell's Florida Gators came within seconds of knocking Georgia out of the National Championship? The RUN AND SHOOT Gangster Pass was Charley's best weapon that day.

Coach Keith Piper at Denison University has worked the RUN AND SHOOT philosophy into his single wing attack with outstanding success.

And Frank Goddard . . . but the list is so everlastingly long . . .

Thousands of new coaches have come upon the scene since *The Offense of the Future* was first published. The great number of requests for the original book has necessitated updating the manuscript and bringing it out as the NOW ATTACK.

Coach, do you realize what this offense can do for you? You can take average material and move the football against anybody. We took a winless bunch of average youngsters who had difficulty grinding out one touchdown per game and turned them into a fire-balling machine that averaged five touchdowns per contest.

Your opponents will have to stretch their defenses thin in order to cover your wide-spread attack, because you will be using all the field. Gang tackling will be difficult and injuries will be reduced to a minimum.

Red-dogging linebackers and blitzing cornermen will "stay at home" after you burn them a few times with Gangster Pass Red-Dog and Gangster Pass Blitz, both of which are automatics.

If you want to put in the LONESOME POLECAT series as a "nuisance" offense, you can cause opposing coaches to sweat out a special defense to cope with it. Even though you may not use the ornery POLECAT in the game, you will have forced your opponent to spend precious practice time preparing for it.

The RUN AND SHOOT OFFENSE is easy to teach. At Ohio State we put in the Kern-to-Jankowski version of the Gangster Pass one week before we were to tangle in the Rose Bowl with John McKay's Trojans led by the awesome O. J. Simpson—and we beat them for the National Championship.

At Lylburn, Georgia, a Little League coach taught his proteges a watered-down version of the RUN AND SHOOT and won the league championship.

Your youngsters will become so motivated with RUN AND SHOOT football that they will get together on their own during the off-season and play aerial in some vacant lot. Average kids will become above-average performers in the exciting art of passing and catching and running and dodging, skills that have made modern football the glamour boy of American sports.

Coach, you will love this offense. Your players will too—so will your fans. Happy touchdown, man!

"Tiger"

CONTENTS

Acknowledgments

There is a progressive little city in southwestern Ohio that holds its head high and constantly looks the world in the eye. Its people keep abreast of changing times. Although they are busy making steel and paper, they focus a watchful eye on their children. If the kids need a new schoolhouse, the townsmen gather at the polls and pass a bond issue and build the schoolhouse. They think that what is good for the youngsters today will be good for the world tomorrow. They are progressive.

In that community lived Elmo Lingrel, as fine a man as I have known, who long ago helped me set the sights and start the firing. Then there was Stan Lewis, whose broad shoulders were always nice to lean on. Harold Mason and Jack Reck made all-state ends of many of our players. Paul Walker took time from his basketball duties to do a great job at the stadium. Ed Payne's fine drive and tireless energy were a source of inspiration to our entire squad. Big Jim Shafor was a tower of strength who handled his strength well.

A fair wind always blew from the administrative office toward the football field because Wade Miller and Russ Baker and Andy Roper occupied the administrative seats, Paul Day, Jerry Nardiello, and Warren Johnson declined bigger newspaper and radio offers elsewhere because they loved the town.

A toast to those men and to this town: "Bon Voyage and happy landings."

Chapter 1

Why We Changed from Possession to Wide-Open Football

Our town was howling and growling. This was the town Jerry Lucas had put on the map as the basketball capital of America. This was one of the first towns to be named *All-American City*. Its great steel mill had never known a strike in its long history. Its paper mill products flowed to every corner of the earth. It was a fine, hard-nosed industrial town. But the entire community was angry. Never in its entire athletic history, which began back in 1911, had the high school football team had a losing season. However, that fine record seemed about to be broken, for this year's team had no victories. It had four defeats, and there was one scoreless tie. With five games left on the schedule the season was exactly half gone. One more defeat would give the town its first losing season in football since time began. I was the football coach.

A SEASON SAVED

"The old coach is over the hill. The years have passed him by. It's time for him to go." The town was unhappy. The coach was perturbed. The football players hung their heads in shame.

Nathaniel Hawthorne once said, "You must begin to hurt if you would become great!" We were hurting, all of us—fans, coaches, and players.

Five weeks later it was the happiest town in the country with the happiest football coach in the world and the proudest players that ever fondled a football. The team had won its last five games and written another winning season into the record books. The Lonesome Polecat had saved the season.

A CHANGE IN OUR FOOTBALL THINKING

We had spent twenty-five years traveling the whole gamut of football offense from Pop Warner's Single Wing to his Double Wing, to the Michigan Short Punt, to the Sid Gillman T, to the Don Faurot T, to Bobby Dodd's Belly T, and had arrived lately at Woody Hayes' Pulverizing T. Through it all our motto was: "Hit 'em so hard and so often with so much that they simply cannot stand up in front of us!" This was serious football. We lifted weights all winter, ran our hearts out all spring, and dug ditches all summer to prepare for the fall grind. Then the Lonesome Polecat came and completely changed our football thinking.

A CRIME AND A SIN AND A SHAME

Average football material in our town meant eight victories and a couple of defeats in one of the nation's toughest interscholastic leagues, where the champion hardly ever went through undefeated. This was a sleepy town toward all things mediocre, but the people woke up and started shouting when the team won more than eight games. They also woke up and started growling when the record showed more than a couple of defeats. That year half the season was gone, and we had posted no victories, four defeats, and a scoreless tie.

Our material was average, perhaps a bit better than average since we had seven regulars returning from a seven-and-three season the year before. There seemed no reason for us to be without victory. No team had ever worked more diligently than we had that year. We hit harder, we ran tougher, we sweat more, and we practiced longer than any team I have ever coached. Still we were winless at mid-season. This was a crime, a sin, a shame—we knew it, felt it, hated it.

AN OFFENSE THAT POPPED

For years it had been our custom every Monday after a one-hour session in front of the locker room blackboard to throw the chalk against the ceiling and roar, "That's our problem for this week—let's get to work!" The players had always bounced to their feet and sprung from the locker room and hurled themselves into their drills. But not that year, not after losing four and tying one and winning none. They pulled themselves slowly to their feet; they dragged themselves sluggishly from the locker room; they went wearily to work. We wanted our boys to love football, but these kids were beginning to hate it.

"When the chips are down and the jig is up and there's hell to pay, *can you pay it?*" We used to bounce back from a defeat with that kind of talk, but after five games and no victories we seemed to have lost our bounce. There was hell to pay all right, and we were behind in our payments.

If a man will picture his problem vividly in his mind, brand it on his brain, drive it into his heart, suddenly during a relaxed moment when the situation seems most hopeless, the right answer will pop. Put a demand on nature and she will supply the need. From out of nowhere one bright fall morning popped the Lonesome Polecat bringing us the right answer.

A SOUL-SATISFYING SEASON

We forgot about work; we began to play. We quit being serious; we commenced having fun. We stopped our blood-and-thunder pep talks; we started telling funny stories. We

laid aside our meat grinder; we took on the Lonesome Polecat. We halted our losing streak; we set into operation a winning streak that went all the way.

So ended the most soul-satisfying season I had known in
thirty years of high school coaching. Our fans acted as if we
had brought them the state championship, our players once
again proudly walked the streets with their heads up, and the
coach began to send forth answers all over the country to
questions asked by high school and college football coaches
about the Lonesome Polecat offense.

Chapter 2

Operation Lonesome Polecat

We do not wish to sell the Lonesome Polecat as a basic offense. That would be a departure into insanity. We used it basically for half a season because we needed to escape from reality, the reality of those first five miserable ball games. We present three plays from the offense, which contained a dozen altogether, to show how the thing served as a stepping stone to the Run-and-Shoot offense that was to average five touchdowns per game at the rate of one touchdown every ten plays for the next four years.

We gave our new formation and all its plays funny names because we wanted to purge our football camp of the graveyard seriousness which had crept into every player and every coach during those first wretched weeks, weeks so miserable that one of our veteran players spent an entire night sitting on a river bank contemplating suicide. I shall be forever thankful that his great strength of character brought him back to our team the next day. Keep in mind a winless team that had come out to win them all in a community steeped in the ways of the winner. We needed to use humor as a tonic for rock bottom morale, hence the humorous names for our plays.

THE LONESOME POLECAT FORMATION

When I drew the new formation on the stadium blackboard before our coaching staff and asked them what we should call our new offense, Stan Lewis, our line coach, replied, "Call it the Lonesome Polecat because it stinks." (Figure 2-1)

The left end lined up 17 yards from the ball always to the open side of the field in an area we called "Heaven," taking with him the left halfback and all linemen except the center, who naturally lined up wherever the ball was in an area designated "Boston." The left halfback took a position right behind the left end. The right halfback and the fullback went always to the closed side, an area we called "Hell," 17 yards from the ball if possible, but never closer to the sideline than 6 yards. These two men lined up a yard and a half behind the line of scrimmage. The quarterback stood erect 11 yards behind the ball. The left end, Roy Lucas, brother of famous basketballer Jerry Lucas, was our captain and best pass receiver and made the decision which was the wide side, while the right halfback acted accordingly, taking the fullback with him to the other side.

NO HUDDLING WITH THE POLECAT

We ran the Lonesome Polecat plays usually without going into a huddle. After the ball was blown dead, Roy Lucas immediately took his group to Heaven and the right halfback, taking his cue from Lucas, went to Hell with the fullback. The center stood behind the ball, facing backward toward the quarterback, whom we called the trigger man. All ten men along the line of scrimmage watched the quarterback until he had flashed the play by using baseball signals. Having called a play, the trigger man then clapped his hands and the center whirled around and took an orthodox stance over the ball, while the others assumed regular three-point stances.

We named the three deep pass-receiving areas Red, White, and Blue because the words have a patriotic ring and patriotism is one of youth's greatest motivating forces. These kids needed motivation. The three short areas designated Heaven, Boston, and Hell opened the way for a bit of com-

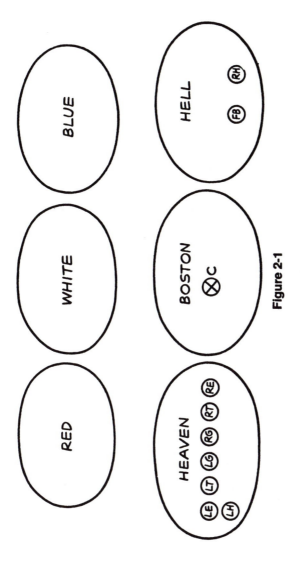

Figure 2-1

7

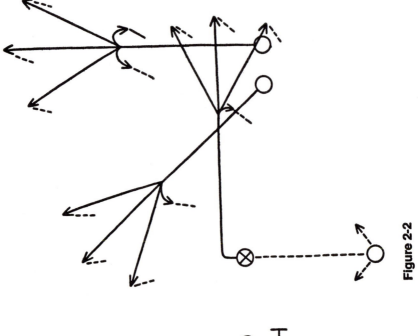

Figure 2-2

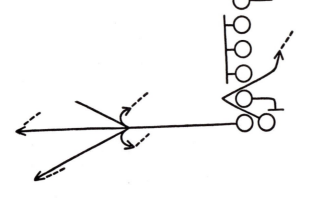

edy when we designated our pass cuts. For instance, "Leave Heaven and go to Boston" and "Spring from Hell into the deep Blue" were a couple of examples.

There were six potential pass receivers, not only the left end, the left halfback, the center, the fullback, and the right halfback but also the quarterback in cases where we put one of the other backs in motion to handle the snap from center.

THE DEAD POLECAT PLAY

Our first play was called the Dead Polecat. The quarterback had the option of hitting any of his five receivers in any of the six areas (Figure 2-2). The pass to Heaven was always the quarterback's first option. If the oponents stationed fewer than five defenders in Heaven, then Heaven was definitely the place to go. It was also the best place for the quarterback to run to when a scramble was on because of the five blockers stationed there. In executing the pass to Heaven, the left end started his cut outside anybody over him so as not to congest the space between the defensive end and the defensive tackle. We wanted this space to be as wide as possible for the left halfback who had to take three steps through this gap and come back between his left tackle and left guard to a point a couple of yards behind his right guard. The left tackle, who had to be an agile blocker, drop-stepped with his outside foot and used a stand-up pass block on the first crasher this side of his left guard. It was absolutely imperative that he stay with his man and ride him to the outside and backward as the play developed. The left guard, the right guard, and the right tackle all set solidly in a shoulder-to-shoulder wall. The right end, another agile blocker, drop-stepped with his inside foot and used a stand-up block on the first crasher this side of the wall, the same tactic employed by the left tackle to the outside. The other pass receivers ran the courses indicated.

The instant the ball left the passer's hand, the left halfback who was still moving toward his spot behind his right guard yelled, "Go!" The word told the blockers on the wall (the left guard, the right guard, and the right tackle) that the pass was on its way and that they were permitted downfield. The left tackle and the right end deftly kept pressure on their men, staying on their feet as long as they could to keep the passing lane free and unencumbered.

After catching the pass, the left halfback drove straight into the wall and took "the daylight" wherever it showed. The continuous movement of the receiver until he caught the ball, first forward through a hole and then backward through another hole, gave the play a look of mobility that prevented the stagnation of a poorly timed screen pass where the receiver stands stock still while the ball is on its way. Such a stagnant pass could be intercepted. Our pass to Heaven was never intercepted.

TRADING ASSIGNMENTS

In order to discourage a defensive lineman from grabbing the left halfback and preventing his return through the hole, we gave the play the variation shown in Figure 2-3. In this variation the left end and the left halfback exchanged assignments. The first time we used this change-up, Roy Lucas went 47 yards for a touchdown. We eventually used the variation as often as the regular maneuver. Lucas called the shot by taking his stance with his left hand behind his tail, showing the left halfback one finger for the regular cut and a closed fist for the variation. The quarterback did not know, nor did he need to know, about the switch in assignments.

POINT OF DECISION

But the pass to Heaven was only the first option the quarterback had on the Dead Polecat play. He could pass to any of the other four potential receivers who ran the courses shown in Figure 2-2. While the snap from center was traveling eleven yards back to the quarterback, we expected each of these four receivers to be five yards into his cut. By the

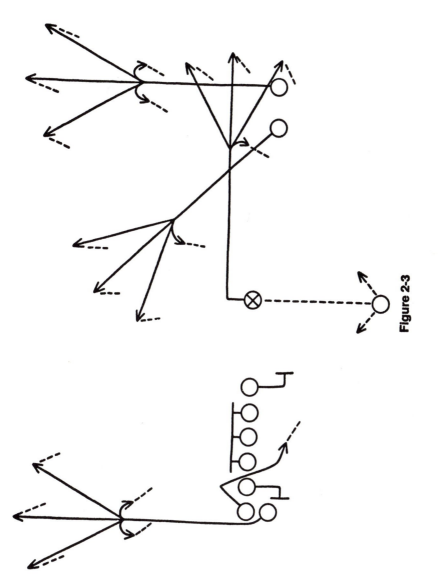

Figure 2-3

11

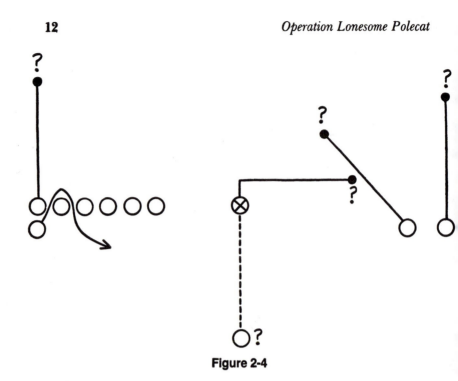

Figure 2-4

time the quarterback had the ball cocked for a pass, the receivers were seven or eight yards along their course, or normally six or seven steps. Therefore we set the fifth step as the "point of decision" (Figure 2-4). By the time he was taking his fifth step, each receiver had to decide one of four things:

1. If he found a defender playing directly in his path and close to him, he broke straight through on his charted course.

2. If he found the defender playing to his right, he broke to the left.

3. If the defender was playing to his left, he broke to the right.

4. If the defender was straight away from him a distance of five yards or more, he hooked right there at the point of decision.

Having made a decision, a receiver had two more steps to start executing that decision. We obligated the quarterback to get the ball started on its way before the receiver had taken more than two steps into his cut so that the defenders could not get a jump on the pass. All five receivers always expected to get the football; however, before the ball was snapped the quarterback decided whom he intended to work with, but he usually did not indicate his intentions to anyone first. If after receiving the snap the quarterback read his chosen receiver clearly at the latter's point of decision, he threw to him immediately from his set position eleven yards back of center. But, if there was any indecision whatsoever, a scramble was on. The quarterback could duck right or left to elude the rushers who seldom numbered more than two men, usually one from each side of center.

WELCOME TO ALL PASS RUSHERS

We welcomed a rush—we invited it by giving absolutely no protection to our passer until a scramble was on. The first time we used the Lonesome Polecat we received a six-man rush. This meant we had ten men up front operating against five. We defeated this formidable opponent 34—0 with a team that had not scored more than twelve points in any of its first five ball games. After that, we usually faced a two-man rush. One team placed the district's two best quarter-milers, a pair of tall boys, at the rush position each side of center. Their best effort resulted in one deflected pass all evening. The harder the rush, the easier it was for the quarterback to scramble right or left to avoid it. Our quarterback was not very fast, but he had a knack for scrambling the last split second before he got clobbered.

When a scramble was on, the five potential receivers jockeyed for an open spot in their own area, except the man in Heaven, who always lit out for Boston (Figure 2-5). Each of the other four, as soon as he saw the quarterback beginning a scramble, re-established his point of decision and ex-

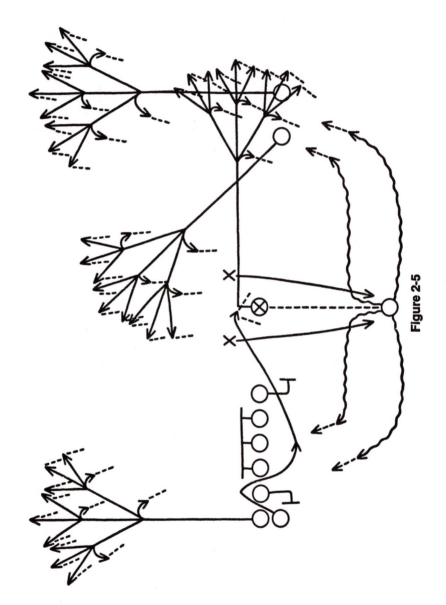

Figure 2-5

ercised one of his four options: he kept going straight ahead or he veered right or he veered left or he hooked where he was—making his choice after a quick look at the position of the defender in his area.

The quarterback knew that during every scramble there would be a receiver in each of the six areas except Heaven. But he knew that Heaven was the best place to scramble to when the opponents were trying to make him eat the ball, because there were five friendly people there eager to work for him.

OTHER TRADE-OFFS

In addition to the trade-off between the left end and the left halfback (Figure 2-3), the Dead Polecat play also had other trade-off possibilities, which were particularly effective against man-for-man defenses. The center could trade cuts with the fullback (Figure 2-6). In making this trade, the center, as he stood facing backward toward the quarterback in his preliminary stance, stuck forth one finger in front of his stomach to indicate to the fullback his intentions. At the snap of the ball each of the two traders ran halfway to his original point of decision and then cut for his co-worker's pass area. All other receivers ran their regular cuts, except that the left end and the left halfback might also be working a trade of their own.

The quarterback paid no attention to all this trading because he knew that there would always be a receiver in each pass area, except Boston in normal situations and Heaven during a scramble. He cared not who it was as long as the fellow wore a friendly jersey.

If the center wished to trade cuts with the right halfback, he held two fingers in front of his stomach as he stood in his preliminary position facing the quarterback (Figure 2-7). Then at the snap of the ball the center and the right halfback broke halfway to their original points of decision, whereupon each headed for his partner's pass area.

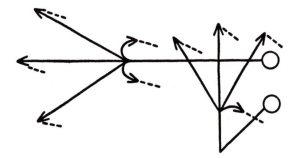

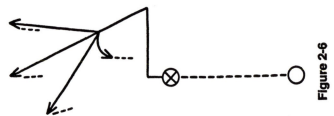

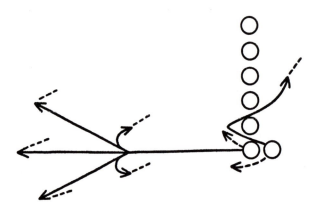

Figure 2-6

16

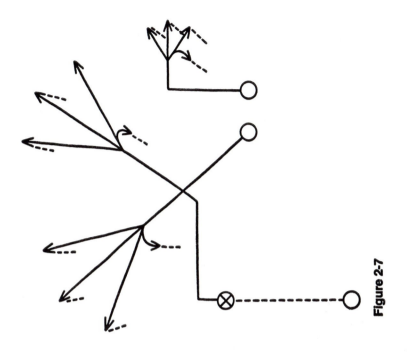

Figure 2-7

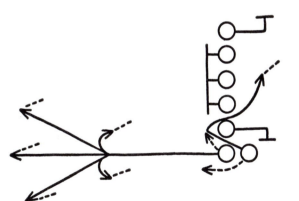

17

With our center trading pass cuts with his fullback or
with his right halfback and with our left end swapping cuts
with his left halfback, all unbeknownst to anybody else, with
our quarterback throwing to whichever of his five receivers
he had a mind to, and with the trigger man throwing the
whole operation into a scramble at any moment of indecision, how could our opponents know what we were up to
when we hardly knew it ourselves? The Lonesome Polecat
operation was always tactical, never strategic.

THE LIVE POLECAT

Remember, we normally called the Lonesome Polecat
plays without going into a huddle. The quarterback from his
deep position flashed baseball signals to indicate Dead Polecat, Live Polecat, Mad Polecat, Polecat Up the River, Cross-
Country Polecat, or any of the twelve plays in our Lonesome
Polecat repertoire. Since we have no intention of selling anybody the Lonesome Polecat as a basic offense but present it
as the crafty fellow who led us to Run-and-Shoot football, we
shall explain only two other Polecat plays—the Live Polecat
and the Mad Polecat.

In working the Live Polecat play, all receivers ran the
same courses as before except the left halfback, who left
Heaven and went to Boston convoyed by the five blocking
linemen breaking straight down the line of scrimmage (Figure 2-8).

All Lonesome Polecat plays went "on the ball" which was
snapped as on a punt without a signal whenever the center
was ready. The other ten men after assuming their stances
kept their eyes on the ball until it was snapped. On the Live
Polecat play the five blocking linemen at the snap of the ball
ran straight down the line of scrimmage with the left halfback running along behind this moving wall. When the men
on the wall heard "Go" shouted by the left halfback the instant the ball left the quarterback's hand, they immediately
turned downfield and threw a block into the first unfriendly
uniform that showed up. They never blocked anyone who

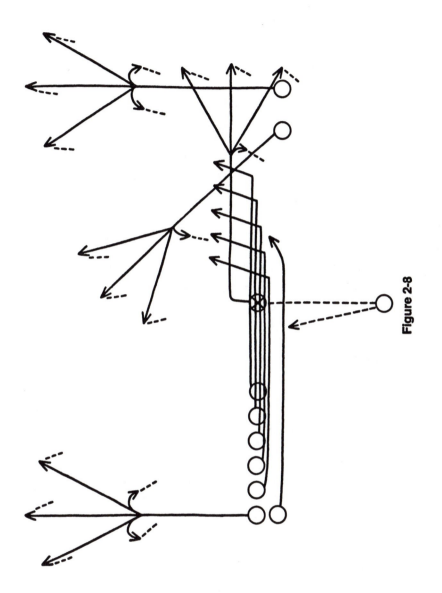

Figure 2-8

19

had crossed the line of scrimmage because the theory of the Lonesome Polecat was that all rushers automatically eliminated themselves from the play. If the quarterback found the lane between him and the left halfback clear, he immediately pushed the ball with a two-handed basketball pass to this receiver who, the moment he caught the ball, turned downfield and took the first daylight that showed. If the quarterback found the lane clogged with enemy personnel, a scramble was on. The moving wall kept running laterally until they heard the barked signal from the left halfback, who never gave this signal until the quarterback turned the ball loose.

LIVE POLECAT SCRAMBLE

Sometimes during a Live Polecat scramble, the convoy moved through Boston and entered Hell before the pass was thrown. Any time the center saw the convoy coming into his pass area during such a scramble, he broke out of Hell and rushed back to Boston (Figure 2-9). As during every scramble on any Polecat play the quarterback knew he had a receiver jockeying in each of the six pass areas except Heaven.

We worked the Live Polecat play one night against a Dayton, Ohio, ball club with Roy Lucas, who had traded assignments with his left halfback (Figure 2-3), going 52 yards for a touchdown without a single block being thrown or a single tackle being attempted, and as Lucas crossed the goal line he was following a big Dayton tackle who seemed to be running interference for him. Organized confusion was the word for the Lonesome Polecat.

THE MAD POLECAT

The purpose of the Mad Polecat play was psychological: we wanted to simulate a scramble to encourage the deep defenders to succumb to the temptation to relax while their teammates clobbered the passer up ahead (Figure 2-10). The

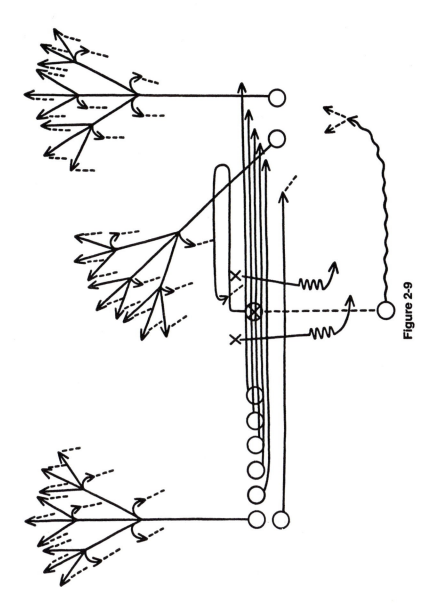

Figure 2-9

21

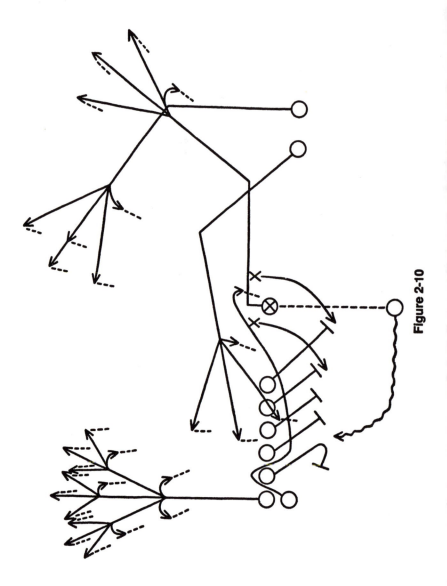

Figure 2-10

22

instant the quarterback got his hands on the ball he headed for Heaven like a scared rabbit heading for his hole. We hoped the defense would begin to drool as the scared rabbit ran for his life. Meanwhile the right end ran back at a 45 degree angle to throw an open field block into the first rusher beyond center. The right tackle rushed back for the first man this side of center. The right guard took the first penetrator who showed this side of his right tackle, while the other guard took the first man this side of his running mate. The left tackle, after his retreat, turned to the outside for the first crasher coming in from the flank. Any blocker who found nobody to block checked his retreat and started forward again taking the first opponent right or left—whichever way was convenient.

The left end took five steps downfield, decided his proper cut, and ran another five steps along that cut while making a new decision. Then he executed the cut that counted and looked for the pass. The left halfback took his usual three steps forward and three more backward. Then he left Heaven and went to Boston. The center, breaking from Boston toward Hell, drove into the deep Blue. The fullback started his break toward the White but then came back toward Heaven hoping to see the pass coming his way. The right halfback began his normal course toward the Blue and then struck out goalward. The pass belonged to any of these five men, or the quarterback could keep on running.

Chapter 3

Lessons Taught by the Lonesome Polecat

The Lonesome Polecat won every game. It completed 63 percent of its passes and had only six intercepted. It got its work done with average material, including both the passer and his receivers, except Roy Lucas who was a great receiver. The quarterback was not fast but he was six feet-three inches tall and he had a knack for scrambling.

After the season the fans acted as if we had won the state championship. Our town went absolutely hog-wild for wide-open football. The Lonesome Polecat set the stage for the Run-and-Shoot offense, which was to become during the next four years the finest way to move a football we had known in thirty years of high school coaching.

Although we bade the Lonesome Polecat goodbye as we became fascinated with our new Run-and-Shoot offense, still we shall be forever indebted to this strange formation for the lessons it taught us in half a season.

SUMMERTIME AERIAL

The Lonesome Polecat taught us that an average passer with average receivers can move the football. Average boys can become better-than-average passers and receivers if their coach will permit them to throw and catch. They will become so motivated that they will get out on their own and play with

24

a football all summer. They will play aerial in the style of the Lonesome Polecat. They will scramble and cut and stop and go, so that they will not need to dig ditches and lift weights and run wind sprints in the summer to get ready for the fall. They will enjoy getting in shape like the basketball players who run and shoot all summer.

MOTION AND EMOTION

We learned that fans love to see a football in motion. We found the air to be the best place for them to see it moving. The older generation will come away from their television sets on Friday nights and Saturday afternoons bringing with them a friend to the ball park to see footballs and human bodies in action. The younger set will flock in droves to the scene where skillful men move with great determination in accordance with a moving ball. The modern fan has whetted his appetite on the pro game which has been piped into living rooms throughout America. This type of game they like, they want, they demand. If we expect to pocket their selective entertainment dollars, we need to give them the exciting style of entertainment they are looking for.

To conclude the point, we decided that since football is a game with a ball in it, we should use the ball, we should let the boys play with the ball, we should put the ball in the air, we should let the people see the ball.

PASSING ON THE RUN

We found while a Polecat scramble was on that a passer can throw on the run as well as he can from a set position. In fact we now know that passing on the run is a more natural maneuver than throwing from set. Each of our Run-and-Shoot quarterbacks came to us rated by their junior high coaches as average passers, but they left our football camp three years later on the all-state team. They all went to college. Those whose college coaches permitted them to run and shoot did a fine job, but those who were made to set up and pass did not fare so well. One of them, possibly the best passer of the lot, gave up football because his coach would not permit him to run and shoot. Yet each of these boys made his all-state team in high school because of his passing, most of which was done on the run.

We discovered that a pass thrown on the run is also more effective than one thrown from set. The running pass is snapped with such a short stroke and with such lightning-like speed that secondary defenders cannot take off with the forward movement of the passer's arm. They are caught with their britches at half-mast. A passer on the run gives a secondary man fits: the deep defender knows not whether the passer intends to run or shoot, whether he as a good defender should rush up and stop the run, or drop back and intercept the pass. He has a problem.

FUN FOOTBALL

The Lonesome Polecat revealed to us that football can be fun and that fun football can win ball games. For years we had kept the squad an hour every Monday before the stadium blackboard cussing and discussing ways and means of annihilating the opponent of the week. But with the coming of the Lonesome Polecat, we became so eager to get out on the field and play aerial with the new offense that we began to take only a few minutes for our scouting report. We decided that scouting reports had been overrated anyway. We began to feel that classroom football taught in the locker room is for the birds—we should do our teaching on the field, for the players had just come from a day-long session in the school house.

While a coach must express his own personality in coaching his boys—he cannot do a great job copying some other coach's emotional stance—still we decided to temper our army-sergeant demeanor and act more like a fond father. We found this to be more fun and certainly more effective because the Lonesome Polecat made every game a winner.

We concluded that *fun* football leads to *optimistic* football which proceeds into *positive* football that gives birth to *winning* football.

Chapter 4

Operation Run and Shoot

The Run-and-Shoot offense was a child of the Lonesome Polecat, but the offspring far surpassed the parent as a basic means for scoring touchdowns. Whereas the Polecat might be called at first glance a departure into insanity, the product of a schizophrenic mind, an escape from reality, the Run-and-Shoot offense made solid sense all the way.

It won thirty-eight games and lost seven in one of the toughest scholastic leagues in America, where the champion seldom went through without a defeat. It averaged almost five touchdowns per game at the rate of one touchdown every ten plays for four years in a row. During that period we punted an average of 1.2 times per contest. One of those years we had the greatest punter in the history of our school—he got to kick the ball only ten times all season.

DEFENSE NEGLECTED

The seven defeats could hardly be attributed to the offense, especially a 36–32 loss or one by a score of 28–26 or another by 22–20. We defeated a charter member of the Greater Ohio League 98–34, which adds up to 132 points scored in a single football game. Where was the defense that night? Actually, where was our defense any night? We found that we had become so fascinated with our new offense that we were neglecting our defense. One major change we would make if we were doing it all over again would be to give the offensive unit 100 percent of its practice time for offense, and the defensive group the same for defense. We would select the eleven best boys for the offensive unit and the second best eleven for the defensive group, feeling that in time the second best boys would be able to do a better job on defense than the number-one offensive group with only a fraction of its time spent on defense. Since this would give us the ultimate in offense backed up by a sound defense, we would therefore have the maximum in football potential.

Coach Chuck Mather of the Chicago Bears had given me this idea years ago while he was coaching at Massillon High School, but even though I nodded in approval, I did nothing about it. I went on using one platoon both ways allowing the boys only about 10 percent of their practice time on defense. Had I used Chuck's idea I believe we could have picked up a few of those seven defeats suffered by the Run-and-Shoot offense through no fault of its own. Possibly the only exception we would make in this plan would be the one or two all-state candidates on the squad, other than the quarterback, who could go both ways, although they would not get more than 10 percent of their time for defensive practice. If I should, after shuffling off this mortal coil, happen to return reincarnated in the form of a high school or a college football coach, I will definitely use Chuck Mather's superb plan: eleven best for offense; next eleven for defense—all the way.

DEFINITION OF RUN-AND-SHOOT

From the opening whistle to the final gun, the Run-and-Shoot offense went for the home run—it tried to score on every play, except for an occasional punt (1.2 punts per game). We refused to punt when the ball rested in front of the 50-yard line. We considered the entire playing field offensive territory. We were willing to pass anywhere on the field on any down.

We made every pass look like a run and every run look like a pass. Offenses that pass from a pocket split their attack into two phases—their running game and their passing game. The setting up of the quarterback in the pocket screams "Pass" to every defender on the field. Even though pocket-passing teams often fake the ball to a runner before setting up in the pocket, still the fake wards off detection for only a moment, after which all defenders spring into anti-aircraft action. The Run-and-Shoot offense did not split its attack—it was just one game, running and passing performed anywhere anytime with no distinguishing clue to signal run or pass.

SAME BLOCKING FOR BOTH RUNNING AND PASSING

All the linemen used the same kind of block whether the play was a run or a pass. There was no cross-field blocking on running plays to tip off a run. Anyhow, our ends were split out too far to get across field on a running play away from them (Figure 4-1). So on every play each end always went downfield toward the defending halfback on his side either to catch a pass, to stalk the deep defender before throwing a block into his lap, or to lure him away from a running play to the other side. We can show you movies of a defensive halfback riding close herd on our faking backside end near one flag while the ball was actually crossing the line of scrimmage on a sweep to the other side. We hurt these secondary defenders so much with sideline passes that they stubbornly refused to believe a run until they saw the ball crossing the line of scrimmage, even though we ran as often as we passed.

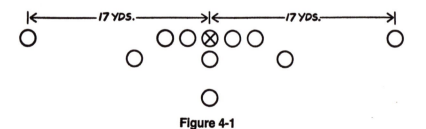

Figure 4-1

SCRAMBLING THE NATURAL WAY

On every pass play the quarterback was free to start a scramble at any moment of indecision on his part or that of a receiver. He naturally got into a scramble whenever his protection broke down. About 10 percent of our passes developed into scrambles; more than that, into near scrambles. In fact we felt we were not ready to launch the season until our trigger man could scramble. But we expected him to be able to scramble the first day of practice. After all, had he not with some of his playmates been spending the entire summer in various sandlots playing aerial à la Polecat, scrambling on his own, having fun getting into shape, learning to scramble the natural way, without some coach standing over him dictating his every move? Only one of our Run-and-Shoot quarterbacks was fast, but they all learned to love a scramble. The very spirit of the Run-and-Shoot offense was "Go reckless, stay loose, and enjoy life."

One of our rival coaches, an excellent three-yards-and-a-cloud-of-dust fellow, cornered me one day after a clinic lecture on the Run-and-Shoot offense and charged me with trying to instill undisciplined progressive education into football. Yet, the year following my departure from high school coaching, this fine possession coach opened up his offense and met my old high school in a 34–34 touchdown parade. I saw the game. I saw that night on that playing field a bunch of kids having more fun with a football than a monkey could with a mile of grapevine. "Go reckless, stay loose, and enjoy life!" Young converts are a great source of satisfaction to an old coach.

SCORING EVENTUALLY vs. SCORING RIGHT NOW

During our possession days we reasoned that, since the offense knew precisely when it was going to move and exactly where it was going to strike, the defense would need a split second to react to the movement and another second or so to determine the point of attack. If our blockers could dig out at this striking point and our ball carrier could dig in behind them, each calling upon every ounce of his energy and every spark of his spirit, then we surely would gain three yards and one foot three times in a row for a first down. Then, if we did not fumble or miss an assignment or get a penalty, eventually we would score. It might take a long time, but sooner or later we were just bound to tally a touchdown. In order not to fumble or crack a signal or get a penalty, we kept the offense simple in those days—we used only a half-dozen or so plays.

We had only one pass play in that old meat-grinder offense. We threw the ball far downfield when we faced a third-down-and-long-yardage situation, expecting to get it intercepted with our nonreceiving receivers tackling the interceptor so that we could tell our fans it was our punt. During those possession days we had to arrive at our opponent's 40-yard line before we considered ourselves in scoring territory. The result was one touchdown for about every 20 plays. This was *simple* football. We won our share of ball games, but our people got a little tired of that kind of football.

With the Run-and-Shoot offense we wanted to score right now. We sought to score on every play. We had a repertoire of about 20 running plays plus a similar number of pass plays. We considered a pass play no better and no worse than a running play—one was as good as the other. We considered the entire playing field scoring territory. We might rifle a pass anywhere anytime, or we might run—it really did not matter which because one maneuver was absolutely *as good as the other*.

If one of our ball carriers fumbled, we said, "So what! Let's score as soon as we get the thing back." If somebody cracked an assignment, we said, "So what! Let's score on the next play." If we received a penalty, we said, "So what! Let's score right now." Maybe you consider this to be Lonesome Polecat thinking. If so, you are absolutely right. This was fun football. The Polecat taught us that *fun* football leads to *optimistic* football which proceeds into *positive* football that gives birth to *winning* football. For proof of the pudding we stuck our thumb into the record book: we found an average of one touchdown every ten plays, five touchdowns per ball game, thirty-eight victories and only seven defeats, and we closed the record book satisfied with Polecat thinking.

SUPPRESSING THE BALL vs. DISPLAYING THE BALL

For many years we hid the football. We hid it from our opponents. We hid it from our fans. We almost hid it from ourselves. The ball was only incidental, a necessary evil that had to be held onto and delivered across yon goal line. "To hell with the ball—let's get to work!" was the cry of our daily practice sessions.

Then for four and a half years we put the ball on display. Though we still tried to hide it from our opponents, we proudly showed it to the fans: they saw it coming through the line; they perceived it sweeping the ends; they got a good look at it traveling the airways. They liked what they saw, and the turnstiles began to click.

WAR OF ATTRITION vs. WAR OF MOVEMENT

Whereas we used to haul forth our heavy armor and throw a siege about our opponent's encampment trying to starve him out and wear him down and force him to surrender after a long war of attrition, now we stretched our legions over a wide front and lashed at the opposition in a war of movement, we discarded our tanks and climbed upon our motorcycles. We found that *motion* on the field created *emotion* in the stands. People came to the ball park.

Chapter 5

The Secret Behind the Run-and-Shoot Offense

The Run-and-Shoot offense forced the defense to spread from hash mark to hash mark. By driving three defenders deep, it broke up the nine-man fronts which had been threatening to stalemate football offenses (Figure 5-1). We used only one formation, a wide double-slot with the ends seventeen yards from the ball but never closer than six yards to the side line and with the interior linemen split two feet apart. The wingbacks were one to three yards from the tackles and one yard behind the line. Thus we had four pass receivers to launch immediately into the secondary where there needed to be at least three deep defenders to cope with them.

A THING OF AMAZEMENT

An amazing thing happened our first two years of Run-and-Shoot football: many of our opponents *refused to spread their deep defenders or come out of their nine-man fronts*. This was great—we put in the Automatic Pass (Figure 5-2).

In executing the Automatic Pass each end, before taking his three-point stance, studied the halfback on his side to determine if this man was over him or inside him. If he found the defender *three yards or more* to his inside, he flashed a baseball signal to the quarterback, who after barking "Set," always checked his ends anytime the defensive halfbacks ap-

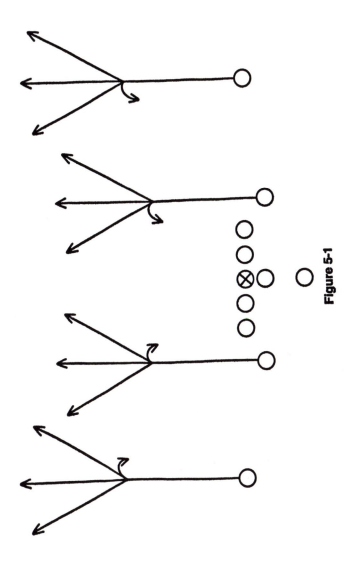

Figure 5-1

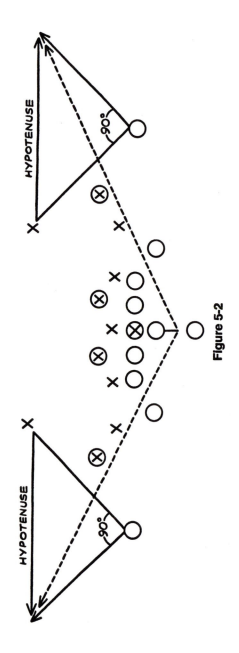

Figure 5-2

peared to be lining up any appreciable distance inside our ends. If the quarterback found one of our ends (or both) still standing and toying with his face bar after the command to set, he read this as a request to "throw me the Automatic Pass." The quarterback signaled for the snap by slapping the center's leg with the back of his hand, and, while all other offensive people waited in their stances for the quarterback's verbal signal that would never come, the trigger man took one step backward with his right foot and rifled the ball to the end over the receiver's *inside shoulder.* The end's course was always taken at a 90 *degree angle* to the inside-positioned defensive halfback.

A bit of elementary geometry will show the receiver running one arm of a right triangle while the defender runs the hypotenuse. Catching the ball over his inside shoulder enabled the receiver to sprint at top speed to the spot of the catch without ever twisting his body or turning his back on the ball. The relationship, geometrically, between the passer and the receiver was simply perfect. This pass was never intercepted—in fact it was deflected only once in four years.

Our split ends looked in at the center snap so that they could get away "on the ball," not only on the Automatic Pass but also on all other plays, for their distance from the signal caller was so great that they sometimes had difficulty hearing him on noisy nights.

The Automatic Pass beat one of our toughest opponents 28–26 in the closing moments of the game after we had completed it nine times out of ten earlier in the contest. They refused to get out of their nine-man front and play our ends head-on. Undoubtedly the easiest ground we ever gained in football came on this simple pass thrown automatically when a defensive halfback refused to play one of our split ends straight away.

HALFBACKS IN MOTION

We started all our plays except the Automatic Pass and an automatic sneak with a halfback in motion—short motion, medium motion, or long motion (Figure 5-3).

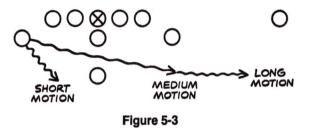

Figure 5-3

On short motion, the ball was snapped when the wingback arrived at a point two yards behind the tackle on his side. On medium motion the snap came when he got to a spot two yards directly behind the other wingback. On long motion the quarterback permitted the moving halfback to get halfway between the other halfback and the split end before calling for the snap. Obviously, we used a nonrhythmic count, the snap being timed with the halfback in motion, whom the quarterback could see from the corner of his eye.

THE AUTOMATIC PASS AS A REGULAR PLAY

Most teams adjusted to this man in motion, especially the medium motion and the long, by rotating their secondary defenders. If we found that in his rotation the man covering our backside end dropped off at least three yards to the *inside,* then the quarterback often called the Automatic Pass in the huddle as a regular play. He called it with long motion to entice the rotating secondary defenders as far as they would go, especially the one covering our backside end (Figure 5-4).

THROWING TO THE BACKSIDE

The side away from the halfback in motion was called "the backside." Since our backside end was usually covered by a single defender in what was practically a man-for-man situation, we began throwing about 20 percent of our passes to this backside receiver. The Lonesome Polecat had proved

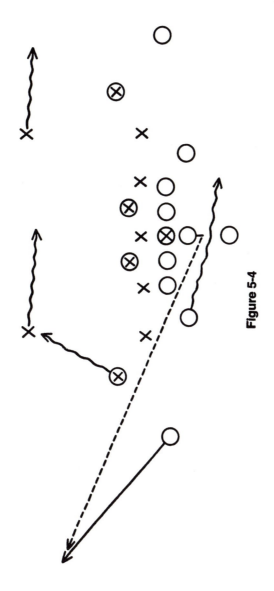

Figure 5-4

39

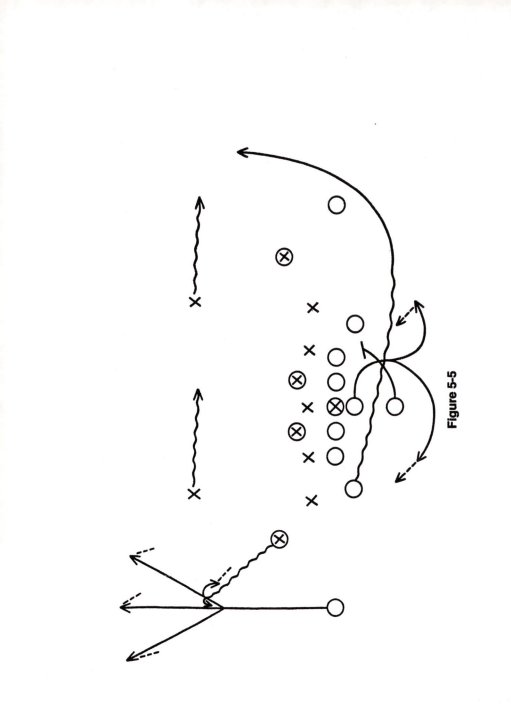

Figure 5-5

to us that a single defender cannot effectively cover a receiver as agile as he is. All passes thrown to a backside receiver were called throwback passes (Figure 5-5). At first our backside end used only the old Polecat rule: If at your point of decision (five steps) you find the halfback playing head on and close, break straight on through—outrun him; if you find him playing to the inside, cut outside; if he plays outside, cut inside; if he is straight away five yards or more, deeper than you, hook right there at the point of decision. Gradually we added to this Polecat maneuver other cuts, which will be explained in a later chapter.

Our earlier quarterbacks "collected up" on their fifth step—they ran to a stop—before those throwback passes, but our last trigger man, Paul Walker, a basketball fast breaker, son of the man who developed Jerry Lucas on the hardwood court, executed a half circle and passed on the run before the backside receiver had taken more than two steps from his point of decision (Figure 5-5). We liked Walker's throwing back on the run better than collecting up and throwing from set because it fit right in with our Run-and-Shoot attitude.

On all plays to the frontside, the man-in-motion side, whether they were passes or runs, the backside end went downfield toward his deep defender to toy with him, to study his reactions, to determine how this man could best be licked on a throwback pass, because we insisted that roughly one of every four plays go to the backside. Always the quarterback checked with his ends in the huddle for advice before calling a throwback pass.

All this attention paid to the backside defensive halfback kept that gentleman out of running plays to the frontside, especially the sweeps, because he discovered that one relaxed moment against our split end could mean a long bomb into his territory.

DEEP DEFENDERS IN A QUANDARY

Imagine the problem the Run-and-Shoot offense gave a secondary defender:

1. He could not anticipate a run or a pass before the ball was snapped because this *strange ball club* passed on any down anywhere on the field.

2. He could not read "pass" when the ends came downfield because these ends always came downfield, run or pass.

3. He could not read "run" from cross-field blocking ends and tackles because these ends and tackles never blocked across field.

4. He could not read "pass" from the quarterback's dropping back into a pocket because this quarterback never set up in a pocket.

5. He could not read "pass" from the set position of pass-blocking linemen because these linemen always fired out, run or pass.

6. He could not read "pass" from the sliding and waiting of backfield pass-blockers because these backs always threw hard-driving blocks on the dead run.

7. He found himself unprepared even with the movement of the passer's arm because the running pass was snapped with such lightning-like speed that the ball was on its way before he could spring into an interception course.

8. If he moved up, there was the long bomb high over his head.

9. If he stayed back, there was the hook pass in front of him.

10. If he moved to the right, there came a pass to his left.

11. If he moved left, there was the ball on the right.

12. If he covered an end on a flag cut, there often went a sweep around the other side.

The defense had problems the like of which they had never known before on a football field. The coach definitely had to work up a special defense for this Run-and-Shoot ball club. Would he be able to teach this special defense during the week prior to the game with the Run-and-Shooters? We were betting that he would not have sufficient time, that even though he might put down his X's in an intelligent array of defensive planning, still his players at game time would find their reactions on the field lacking in that spontaneity so vital in killing an offense. One touchdown every ten plays for four years proved we were right.

Just imagine the tremendous progress in football if every coach would stop being a copycat and start calling upon his imagination for new offensive ideas as did old-timers Bob Zuppke and Pop Warner and Knute Rockne, to name only a few.

DOUBLE-COVERAGE TABOO

With three men forced deep, the flat defenders could not afford to help the defensive halfbacks double-cover *both* our split ends (Figure 5-6). Such double-coverage would leave only a six-man front facing our close-knit nine-man offense. We ran inside all night against one ball club that persisted in double-covering both our ends.

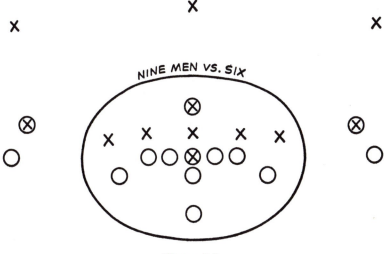

Figure 5-6

GOODBYE TO GANG TACKLING

The greatest weapon carried by a defensive football team is the gang tackle. The late Bear Bryant of the University of Alabama probably did the greatest job in modern football in motivating his young men to gang up on a ball carrier and make the lad sorry he had not gone out for waterboy. If Alabama failed to smash eleven vicious shoulders into a leather-lugger, the old Bear was unhappy. We found that the Run-and-Shoot offense broke up gang tackling. It prevented eleven defenders from starting on a pursuit course at the snap of the ball because they were not sure whether the play was a run or a pass until the ball crossed the line of scrimmage. By forcing three defenders deep and stretching the entire defense hash mark to hash mark, the offense gave a ball carrier lots of daylight in which to maneuver. When he was tackled, the whistle blew before many tacklers could get a piece of him because some of these defensive people had to come from such a long way off. During the four years of the Run-and-Shoot and the half-year of the Lonesome Polecat, we had only one football player fail to bounce to his feet the moment the whistle blew. We concluded that wide-open football minimizes injuries by eliminating gang tackling.

THE RUN-AND-SHOOT REPERTOIRE

We used five series of plays with hardly a change in a single play for the entire four years. In spite of the fact that the coaches in the Greater Ohio League exchanged movies and our offense was known to our rivals about as well as to ourselves, we scored 60 touchdowns the last year, 26 of them by way of the air.

One of our chief rivals sent its scouts down one night with our plays already drawn upon a clipboard before the game even started. When asked why they bothered to scout us, one of them replied, "Oh, we know all your plays—we just came down to keep tab on how many times you call each play." They wanted to study our tendencies. Actually, we let the defense determine our tendencies. Just how this worked will be explained later.

The Run-and-Shoot offense consisted of five series of plays:

The Gangster

The Cowboy

The Wagon Train

The Popcorn

The Mudcat

Calling a play by an expressive name instead of a number was a carryover from the Lonesome Polecat, for we decided to keep on having fun, although we thought we might refrain from being downright ridiculous. Even so, there may really be nothing ridiculous about any procedure that brings home a victory.

Chapter 6

Ordering the Defense

In order to understand the Run-and-Shoot offense you need to know how we numbered the opponent's defensive men. We executed most of our plays by singling out one specific defender and letting him tell us what to do either by the place where he lined up before the ball was snapped or by his movement after the snap. We used the baseball batter's idea, "Hit where they ain't," rather than the old football possession slogan, "Git there fustest with the mostest!"

You are already familiar with the simple Polecat thought which directed a pass receiver to veer right or left or go straight ahead or hook, depending on what his defender told him to do (Figure 2-2). We retained this thinking for some of our Run-and-Shoot passes. You recall how on the Polecat scramble each of four receivers re-established his point of decision and started over again (Figure 2-5). We kept this same thought during every Run-and-Shoot scramble.

NUMBERING THE DEFENDERS

But in the Run-and-Shoot offense we went much further with this type of thinking, most of it—I repeat, *most of it*—based on what one specific defensive man told us to do. Therefore it is absolutely necessary that you know the label we placed on each defensive man. All defenders to the side of our man in motion were named Frontside Defenders and all those away from motion Backside Defenders (Figure 6-1). We gave them capital letters because they represented major problems in our struggle for existence. Anybody directly over our center was Number Zero. Anybody right behind Number Zero, otherwise the first man to the motion side of him, was designated Frontside One; the next, Frontside Two; then in order, Frontside Three, Frontside Four, and Frontside Five. At this point we expected to start over with Backside Five, Backside Four, Backside Three, Backside Two, and finally Backside One.

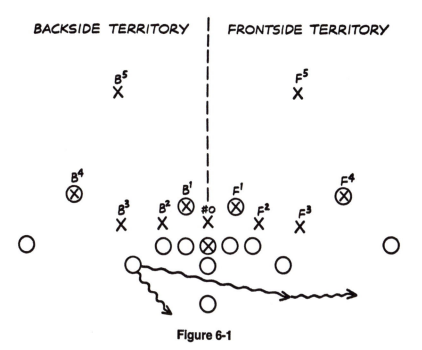

Figure 6-1

UNWELCOME STRANGER

However, there were nights occasionally when an Unwelcome Stranger suddenly showed up in Frontside Territory (Figure 6-2). Whenever this happened, lights went on and bells rang in the quarterback's brain while a big sign flashed on his mental blackboard: "We'll be hitting the back-side tonight!" We called this Unwelcome Stranger *Frontside Six.* Against this overload we felt we must strike at least 50 percent of our time away from motion. Normally we oper-ated away from motion about 25 percent of the time.

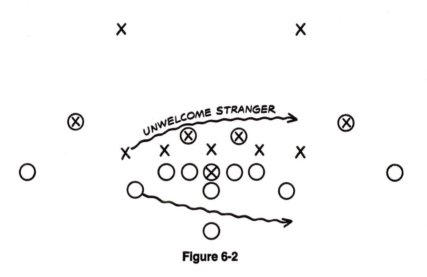

Figure 6-2

LOOKING AT A NORMAL DEFENSE

We expected that by the time our halfback in motion arrived at the snap point on medium and long motion plays, there would be a deep middle defender, whom we would still call Backside Five (Figure 6-3). So long as this man did not get more than three yards into Frontside Territory before the ball was snapped we remained calm and continued to designate him Backside Five. However, if this fellow consist-ently came flying into Frontside Territory more than three yards, then he became an Unwelcome Stranger known spe-cifically as Frontside Six, and we knew our Throwbacks and Counters were in for a busy evening. However, we were still confident that the good old reliable Gangster Series would continue to move the ball on the frontside even with the Unwelcome Stranger in our midst.

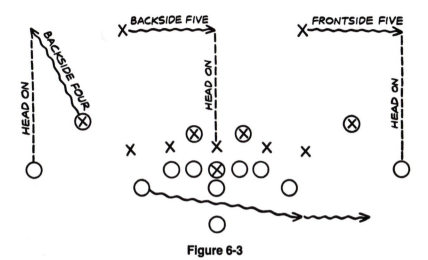

Figure 6-3

Chapter 7

Frontside Gangster

The Gangster was the first series we worked on each day, for it was one of our two most popular operations. The series had unlimited possibilities, and the temptation to keep creating plays was great, but we finally disciplined ourselves to only those Gangster plays explained in the next two chapters because we did not want more offense than we could practice in one day. We went through our entire five-series repertoire every day. We were absolutely sure that this complete coverage of the entire offense each practice session was a basic principle demanded by every offense that features the ball on display. We wanted to become so adept at handling the football that we could put on a skillful exhibition blindfolded. Besides, handling the ball was fun, and we were playing fun football (because *fun* football was *winning* football).

GANGSTER PASS RIGHT

All Gangster plays went either on medium or on long motion (Figure 5-3). Whenever the quarterback in the huddle said, "Gangster Pass Right" (or left), nobody in the lineup knew which one of five possibilities was about to be developed: the Automatic Pass, the Gangster Blitz, the Gangster Red-Dog, the Gangster Walkaway, or the Gangster Scramble in which the trigger man would either throw his ears back and run like a scared rabbit or toss a mad-dog pass to any of four receivers Polecat style. These five possibilities will be explained in the order mentioned.

TOP BILLING FOR THE AUTOMATIC PASS

The first possibility on any Run-and-Shoot play was always the Automatic Pass to the backside end, the end away from the play called in the huddle (Figure 5-2). After ordering the team at the line of scrimmage to set, the quarterback looked at the backside defensive halfback to determine whether or not the fellow was playing three yards or more inside our backside end. If this deep defender appeared guilty of such alignment, the quarterback glanced at his backside end to see if he was still standing after the command to set and playing with his face guard, which was his way of signaling for the Automatic Pass. If the end was showing this signal, the quarterback could at his own discretion, by slapping the center's leg, take the snap silently and throw the Automatic Pass; or he could go on through with the play called in the huddle, in this case Gangster Pass Right.

GANGSTER PASS BLITZ

If there was no signal flashed by the backside end calling for the Automatic Pass, or if the quarterback chose to ignore such a signal, then the trigger man, as he set for Gangster Pass Right, looked to his right to locate the position of Frontside Four. Was he in the Blitz position, the Walkaway position, or the Hardnose position? (Figures 7-1, 7-2, 7-3.) Where would he be when our halfback went in motion? What position would he occupy—the Blitz or the Walkaway or the Hardnose? That was the sixty-four dollar question.

If he took up the Blitz position, the quarterback would throw the Blitz Pass, a quick pass snapped on his third running step to his frontside end breaking on a look-in course (Figure 7-4). He started this play like all his plays, except the Automatic Pass and the Automatic Sneak, by speaking any

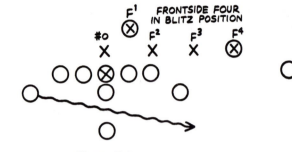

Figure 7-1

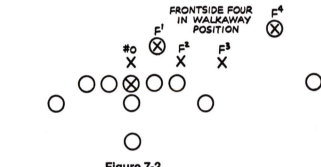

Figure 7-2

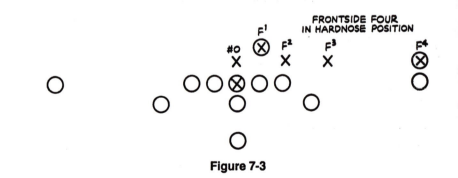

Figure 7-3

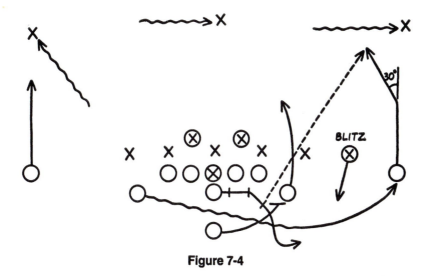

Figure 7-4

double-digit number to set the left halfback in motion. This
man in motion passed between the quarterback and the fullback, and as he went by he tapped the quarterback on the tail
with the back of his hand to let the trigger man know where
he was. At the moment of the tap the quarterback looked to
his right at Frontside Four, simultaneously seeing the man in
motion out of the corner of his eye. When the moving halfback arrived at a spot two yards behind his right halfback,
the trigger man barked the snap signal and, opening with a
short lead step, took two steps straight down the line followed by a third step diagonally backward. Just as his right
foot hit the ground on this third step, he whipped a quick
pass to the right end.

There was no setting up for the snap throw—he passed
on the run, permitting his feet to carry him a few more steps
diagonally backward after the throw. His entire body was
loose and free-wheeling during the entire maneuver. He executed the play like a man who owned the world. He moved
with confident, positive poise as if he had completed this pass
a thousand times before. Maybe he had, during the summer,
with no coach to bother him.

Here is an important point in Run-and-Shoot football: A passer running backward can throw a football forward if the pass is not intended to be longer than ten yards; on longer passes he must get himself turned downfield as he passes the ball. This point will be dwelled upon later.

On this Blitz Pass our right end, having seen Frontside Four assuming the Blitz position, looked in at the ball as he crouched in his three-point stance with his outside foot back. Getting off with the snap and taking three steps straight downfield, he planted his right foot on his third step and cut in at a 30 degree angle so that he was running away from the line of scrimmage at an angle of 60 degrees. He ran under control until he caught the ball about seven or eight yards downfield. He was prepared for the catch with his chest turned squarely toward the passer so that he could reach left or right or up or down wherever the ball was thrown.

Since the passer threw on his third running step to the end cutting on his third step, the pass was thrown almost exactly at the moment of the receiver's cut to the inside. We had learned that short passes should be thrown instantaneously with this break, or as close thereto as possible. The Polecat had taught us that longer passes could be thrown effectively after the receiver had taken a couple steps into his cut.

GANGSTER PASS RED-DOG

This quick, three-step snap of the football by the quarterback going to the right (four steps going left) served a vital purpose other than dealing with Frontside Four in the Blitz position. It became a natural automatic, known as Gangster Pass Red-Dog, whenever an inside linebacker was crashing to the side of the motion—a maneuver quite popular with some of our opponents (Figure 7-5).

If the quarterback, stepping along the line after calling Gangster Pass Right in the huddle, sensed a blitzing interior linebacker pouring in on him from the frontside, he arched the ball on his third step to the right halfback five yards

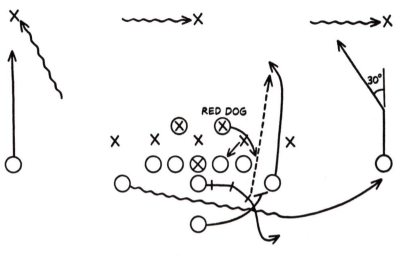

Figure 7-5

straight over the line. The right halfback, who always studied this linebacker on every Gangster Pass, expected, the moment he saw the linebacker crash, to receive the ball over his inside shoulder about five yards straight ahead. Even though he sometimes had to fight his way out past Frontside Three, still he knew his job was immediately to get out and down to the spot. Again this maneuver was automatic whenever a frontside interior linebacker crashed against our Gangster Pass. Only the passer and the receiver knew this particular phase of the Gangster Pass was developing.

Now then, hold on to your seat: there was one more wrinkle in the Red-Dog Pass. This whole series of possible maneuvers on the Gangster Pass was much simpler in the doing than it is in the telling. Here was the other wrinkle (Figure 7-6)): If our right halfback saw his key linebacker coming in motion along with our man in motion, he knew again that his job was to catch the Red-Dog Pass but with one exception—he was now to catch it over his *outside* shoulder in order to keep the pass away from the other linebacker who might have moved into the middle when his partner went in motion. This phase of the Gangster Pass was another private matter between the quarterback and the right halfback. An

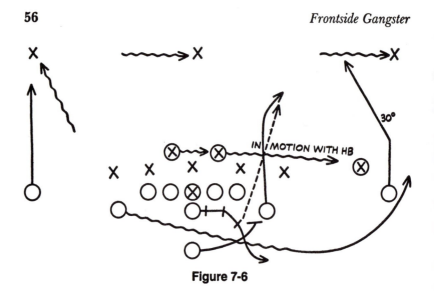

Figure 7-6

important coaching point here is that the quarterback permitted his halfback in motion to proceed on long motion halfway to the split end before calling the snap number so that the linebacker would get out of position as far as he was willing to go.

GANGSTER PASS WALKAWAY

The fourth possibility after Gangster Pass Right had been called in the huddle was the Gangster Pass Walkaway. Here the quarterback, after setting his men in their stances and seeing no signal for the Automatic Pass from his left end, found that when he put his left halfback in motion, Frontside Four was staying back in the Walkaway position. The Walkaway Pass was now on the fire (Figure 7-7). As before, the quarterback's first two steps were straight down the line before starting his diagonal movement backward. During these first two steps, of course, he was reasonably watchful for a crashing linebacker. Obviously, such a red-dogger would have caused him to throw the Red-Dog Pass. But, from his third step on, he studied Frontside Four because this man was going to tell him whether to throw the football

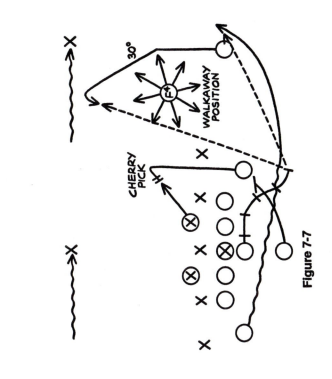

CHERRY PICK

WALKAWAY POSITION

30°

F.L.

Figure 7-7

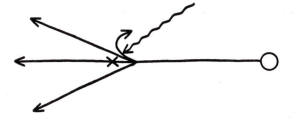

to the halfback in motion or to the hooking end. We wanted
Frontside Four properly read by the time the quarterback
took his fourth step, for the ball needed to be thrown on his
fifth step. Here was the trigger man's thinking as he moved
backward on his third and fourth steps:

1. "He left—I right," meaning that if he found during his third and fourth steps that Frontside Four
   was moving left in the Walkaway position (passer's
   left), the pass should be thrown to the right to the
   halfback in motion.

2. "He right—I left," meaning that if he found
   Frontside Four moving right in the Walkaway position, the pass should be rifled to the left to the
   end hooking.

3. "He up—I back," meaning that if Frontside Four
   was moving up from the Walkaway position, the
   pass should be thrown behind him to the hooking
   end.

4. "He back—I up," meaning that if Frontside Four
   was moving back in the Walkaway position, the
   pass should be thrown in front of him to the
   halfback.

Lateral movements took precedence over movements forward and backward; i.e., if Frontside Four was *up and right,*
the pass was thrown toward the *left* to the end; if Frontside
Four was *up and left* the pass was thrown toward the *right* to
the halfback. The same rule held for movements *back and left,*
and *back and right.* The point to remember is that *right* and *left*
were more important than *up* and *back.*

The right end knew automatically on Gangster Pass
Right, when he saw Frontside Four staying back in the
Walkaway position after our halfback went in motion, that
his job was to take three steps straight downfield, plant his
right foot on his third step and cut to the inside at an angle of
30 degrees the same as on the Blitz Pass. But now he looked

for the ball on his *fifth* step because the quarterback was snapping the pass on his own *fifth* step, either to the end or to the man in motion, depending on what Frontside Four had influenced the quarterback to do. If the end found the pass directed at him, he took two more short, quick collect-up steps (steps six and seven), stopped, turned, and played first base as the ball sped toward him. We felt absolutely sure that a hook-pass receiver should always take these two little collect-up steps *after* the pass was released—that he should still be moving forward at the moment of release—so that a deep defender could not get a toe-hold on the play and spring forward to intercept or deflect.

If the end found the pass headed laterally toward the halfback in motion, he broke away from his hook toward the sideline to throw a block on Backside Five, leaving it up to his left halfback to get rid of Frontside Five the way a good ball carrier should always eliminate the first tackler in the open field (Figure 7-8).

If the quarterback found after he had set his halfback in motion that Frontside Four had come up and stationed himself in the Hardnose position in front of our right end, we figured he would still walk away and cover either our end or our halfback in motion; so, we still planned to throw the Walkaway Pass. We had a play, explained later in this chapter, called Gangster Pass Hardnose that we liked for a Frontside Four who consistently hardnosed our frontside end.

CHERRY-PICKING HALFBACK

On the Gangster-Pass-Right call, the right wingback was either a pass receiver or a "cherry-picker." The first linebacker this side of center, otherwise the middle linebacker, told him what to do. Here was his thinking:

1. "He red dog—I catch inside," meaning that if the linebacker tried to crash through our line, our

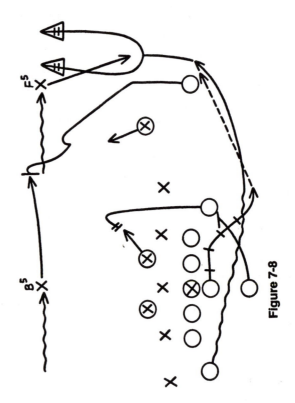

Figure 7-8

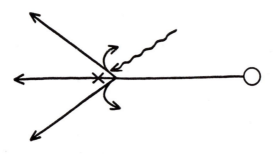

right wingback would look for the Red Dog Pass over his inside shoulder five yards straight ahead (Figure 7-5).

2. He come—I catch outside," meaning that if this linebacker went in motion with our man in motion, our wingback would look for the same pass but over his outside shoulder (Figure 7-6).

3. "He stay—I cherry-pick," meaning that if the linebacker stayed at home, our wingback would go to a spot between the linebacker and the area where our right end would hook (Figure 7-7). Here he would spread his feet and permit the linebacker to run into his basketball cherry-pick as the defender was backing off to guard the hook zone.

The only time the officials ever called this move illegal was when one of our sophomore halfbacks lowered his shoulder and clobbered the linebacker. We expected our cherry-picker to spread his feet, cross his raised arms over his chest, and catch the linebacker as the poor fellow jolted into him. Surely a harmless basketball cherry-pick, often used in the non-contact sport, could not be termed unsportsmanlike in the rough and rugged sport of American football. We used it because it enabled us to charge down upon Frontside Four in his Walkaway position with a basketball fast break, two on one, our man in motion to his outside and our hooking end to his inside.

THINKING ALONG WITH THE QUARTERBACK

Before discussing the Scramble Play which was always the last resort on any play in our offense, let's review briefly the quarterback's thinking on Gangster Pass Right, because this play with its flexibility in the ball handling can be a beautiful thing, a work of art, poetry in motion:

1. The quarterback in the huddle calls Gangster Pass Right.

2. At the line he commands his team to set as he looks to his left end for the sign of the Automatic Pass.

3. Getting the sign, he can throw the Automatic, or he can go on with the play called in the huddle.

4. In going on, he barks any double digit number to start his left halfback in motion.

5. Feeling the halfback's tap on his tail, he looks to the right at Frontside Four but simultaneously sees his moving halfback from the corner of his eye.

6. The instant the left halfback arrives at a point two yards behind his right halfback, the quarterback barks the snap signal.

7. If he has found Frontside Four lined up in the Blitz position he moves down the line ready to throw the Blitz Pass on his third step. The right end is prepared for the pass because he too has noted the position of Frontside Four.

8. If, however, during his first two steps down the line, he senses an interior linebacker crashing to the frontside, he automatically throws the Red-Dog Pass by laying the ball on his third step five yards straight ahead of his right halfback, who expects it when he sees the linebacker crash.

9. If, before he even starts down the line, the trigger man senses the interior linebacker going in motion along with our man in motion, he calls the snap number on long motion and again throws the Red-Dog Pass but this time over the outside shoulder of the right halfback, who again has taken his cue from his key linebacker.

10. If the quarterback has found Frontside Four either in the Walkaway position or the Hardnose po-

sition, he moves down with the idea of throwing the Walkaway Pass on his fifth step either to the right end or to the left halfback, depending on the movement of Frontside Four.

Figure 7-9 illustrates these movements in diagram form, rather a complicated look for the defense but really a simple maneuver for the offense: if you let the kids play with the football; if they go home for their summer vacation motivated by the knowledge that you believe in this sort of thing; if they spend their summer tossing the ball around à la Lonesome Polecat.

GANGSTER PASS LEFT

In working the Gangster Pass Left with a right-handed quarterback, there were unavoidably a few slight differences from Gangster Pass Right:

1. Instead of three steps on Gangster Pass Blitz and Gangster Pass Red-Dog, the quarterback took four steps; instead of five steps on the Walkaway, he took six; and instead of seven on the Hardnose (Figure 7-23, to be explained later), he required eight—in short, the passer needed one more step going left than he did moving right, because with right-handed passers, coordination required the ball to start backward the moment his left foot hit the ground and forward the instant his right foot hit.

2. Since our ends lined up with their outside feet back, which meant they would always start forward with their outside feet first, the left end on Gangster Pass Blitz would look for the ball on his fourth step, which was his first step to the inside, rather than the instant of his cut on his third step as the right end had done.

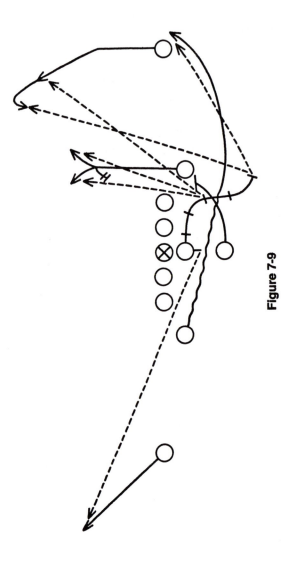

Figure 7-9

64

However, these slight differences did not muddy up the pond—they did not cut down on the efficiency of the passing attack to the left.

GANGSTER SCRAMBLE

The last possibility on the Gangster Pass Right was the Gangster Scramble. It occurred when there was indecision on the part of the quarterback caused by a receiver's not getting out or a breakdown in protection or somebody's failure to read a key correctly. At any rate if the quarterback on his fifth or seventh step found himself running with the ball still in his hands undecided where to throw, he could keep running to the frontside or he could whirl and circle to the backside. We told him we would never be mad at him as long as he got the ball back to the line of scrimmage.

As soon as the receivers sensed a scramble was on, each quickly checked the defender in his area and made a new decision: if the defender was directly in his path and close to him, he ran right on through trying to get beyond him; if the defender was on his right, he broke to the left; if the man was on his left, he broke to the right; and if the fellow was dead-ahead at least five yards, he hooked right there at the point of decision (Figure 7-10). We asked the frontside wingback to rush to the Lonesome Polecat's Heaven or Hell (Figure 2-1), depending on the side to which the quarterback was scrambling. After making their initial blocks, the linemen always jumped to their feet and checked for a scramble, rushing down the line toward the side the quarterback was scrambling to.

SPECIAL FOR UNWELCOME STRANGERS

Back in Figure 6-2 we illustrated an Unwelcome Stranger, whom we called Frontside Six, showing up in Frontside Territory. Even though this overload toward our motion side normally dictated that we hit to the backside away from

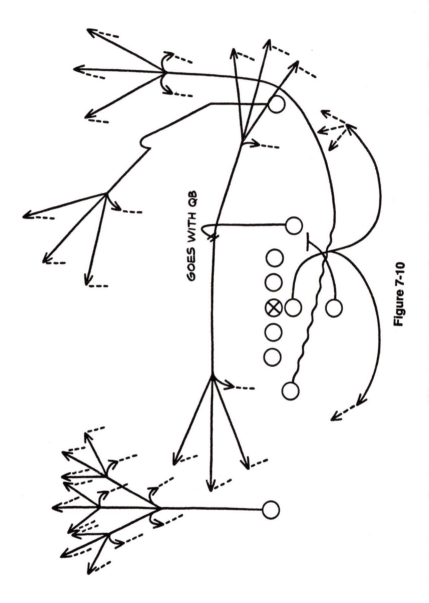

GOES WITH QB

Figure 7-10

66

motion, we devised a special play to entertain the Unwelcome Stranger on the frontside. But first we needed to know what this Frontside Six had come over to do. We found him doing one of two jobs: (1) Sometimes he rode close herd on the man in motion to stop the flare pass to this receiver on Gangster Walkaway, leaving Frontside Four to drop off and break up the hook pass to the end (Figure 7-11). (2) At other times he turned the man in motion over to Frontside Four while he himself dropped off to cover the hook (Figure 7-12).

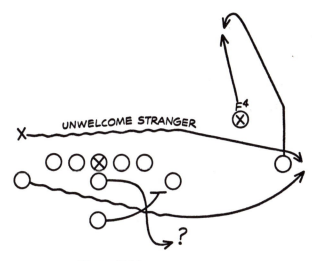

Figure 7-11

If we happened to meet an Unwelcome Stranger while working the Walkaway Pass, our quarterback was in for a moment of indecision, from which he probably would try to extricate himself tactically by starting a scramble that would most likely wind up with a throwback to the backside end. So we devised a special play for this unusual situation, a play we called Gangster Walkaway Special (Figure 7-13).

Our wingback took his maximum split of three yards from his tackle, so that he would have plenty of room to cherry-pick the oncoming Frontside Six whose motion was

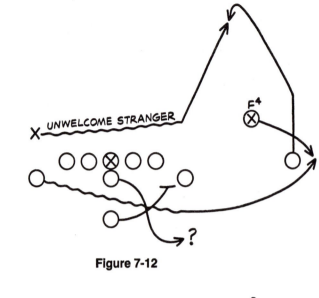

Figure 7-12

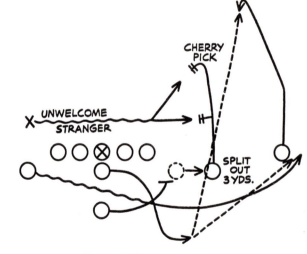

Figure 7-13

paralleling that of our halfback in motion. The quarterback
spat out the snap signal a moment sooner than normal, actually at the instant our halfback in motion arrived behind his
frontside tackle, so that our wingback would have plenty of

time to get to his cherry-picking spot. Now, if Frontside Six kept coming straight, our right halfback with his feet spread in the man's path caught him in a cherry-pick; if this defender in motion started dropping off toward the hook zone, our cherry-picker got there first. Now, our quarterback was in business as usual, throwing the pass wherever indicated by Frontside Four.

BLOCKING FOR THE GANGSTER PASS

Since we did not want our opponents to know whether we were running or passing we used the same type of block for runs as for passes. Against hard-nosing linebackers the blocking was as shown in Figure 7-14.

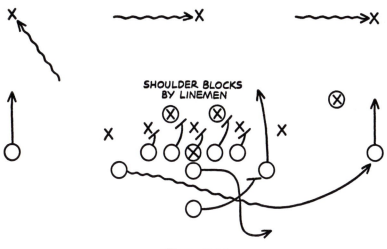

Figure 7-14

Against soft linebackers, as in the 3-4 defense, each guard took a jab step forward to seal the hole. Finding it sealed, the backside guard would drop back and look outside for a blitz, while the frontside guard would help his center against Number Zero (Figure 7-15).

Against the 4-3 defense, our center would first seal the hole and then drop off for a backside blitz (Figure 7-16).

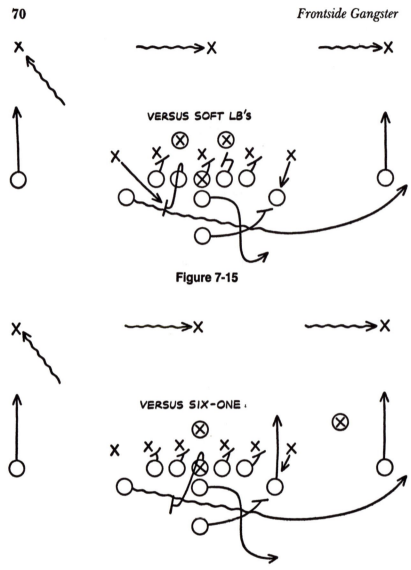

VERSUS SOFT LB's

Figure 7-15

VERSUS SIX-ONE

Figure 7-16

The fullback's block was extremely important. The Run-and-Shoot offense was absolutely no place for a fullback who did not like to hit people. We wanted the fullback to spring from his three-point stance, in which his feet were always parallel, and aim his inside shoulder at the far knee of Frontside three. These were his coaching points:

1. Break his far leg by driving your inside shoulder through it knee high. (For the benefit of fond football mothers we hasten to explain that by "break his leg" we meant "hit it so hard that it flies back." I do not recall that we ever broke anybody's leg with this block.)

2. Hook his near leg with your inside leg.

3. Turn your body straight downfield as you drop to all fours.

4. Dig him downfield five yards.

5. Make him escape to the backside.

This same block was used by our halfbacks on the Cowboy Pass to be discussed later. This was also our open-field block. We used it as one of our warm-up exercises before every practice and before every game, going through the exercise at half-speed and emphasizing all five coaching points. In actual game conditions the first coaching point was usually as far as the blocker got because throwing his shoulder into a defender with all the force he could muster normally took the man to the ground.

Coach Lowell Storm of Springfield South High School, Springfield, Ohio, and later with the Los Angeles Rams, a fine coach who gave us more trouble with his defensive end play than any coach we have ever faced, said that the thing about the Run-and-Shoot offense that bothered him most was the vicious block of our fullback on Gangster passes and our halfbacks on Cowboy passes. The block was an absolute "must" in our offense.

QUARTERBACK ALONG THE LINE

There were three reasons in Gangster plays for having our quarterback traveling straight down the line on his first two steps:

1. His movement along the line would set up the full-back's block on Frontside Three (Figure 7-17).

2. This lateral movement would enable our quarter-back easily to check for a linebacker crashing after the ball was snapped (Figure 7-5).

3. The movement was absolutely imperative to set up Frontside Three for the Gangster Run.

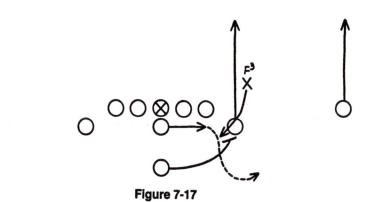

Figure 7-17

GANGSTER ON THE RUN

Whenever we could come up with a fullback with speed, we got a lot of mileage from Gangster Run, right or left (Figure 7-18). The linemen used the same hard-driving block they employed on the Gangster passes. The play was highly optional. We expected the quarterback coming straight down the line for two steps as on Gangster passes to shorten his third step, his diagonal step backward, as he studied Frontside Three. This third step was his point of decision: if Frontside Three angled toward him, he pitched a one-

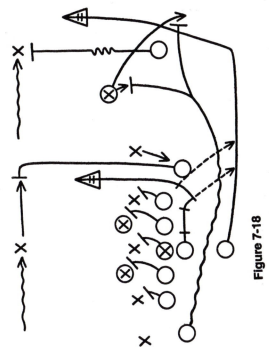

Figure 7-18

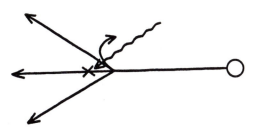

handed flip pass to the wide-running fullback; if Frontside
Three came straight across, he faked the pitch to the fullback
as he drove off his right foot straight upfield; if Frontside
Three just stood there on the line, he pushed off his right
foot straight into this defender and lateraled the ball to the
fullback a couple yards wider. There were two important
coaching points on this play:

1. The quarterback had to call the snap signal an instant before the man in motion arrived behind the
   wingback, actually when he arrived behind the
   tackle. The danger was that the moving halfback
   might get so far ahead of the fullback that his
   block on Frontside Four would come too soon for
   the ball carrier to take advantage of it.

2. The left halfback had to run under control as he
   approached Frontside Four—he had to stalk his
   man—so that the fullback could stay within four
   yards of his interferer and use the block properly
   when it came.

If the quarterback, as he shoved off his right foot,
sensed that Frontside Two was flowing to the outside, he
drove inside this man (Figure 7-19). If he noticed before the
ball was snapped a Frontside-One linebacker sneaking up
with blood in his blitzing eye, he could, after the initial step
with his right foot, drive up inside this man (Figure 7-20). If
he had been getting a consistent veer to the motion side by
Number Zero, he might after the initial step drive to the
backside of his center (7-21).

All the possibilities prevalent when Gangster Run Right
was called in the huddle are illustrated by Figure 7-22. To
repeat—our Gangster Run was highly optional.

THE HARDNOSE PASS

We had a special pass for a Frontside Four who consistently stepped up and assumed the Hardnose position on our
frontside end (Figure 7-23).

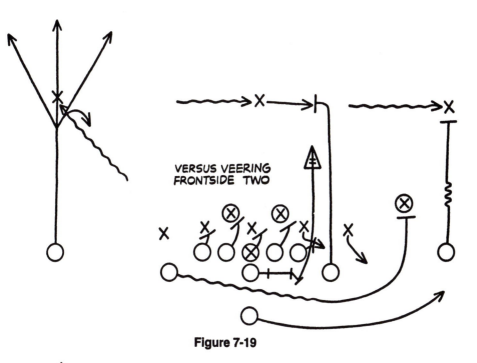

Figure 7-19

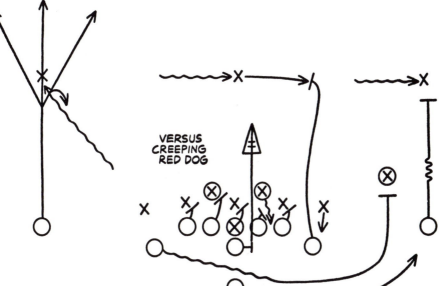

Figure 7-20

We had no way of working it automatically while the Gangster Pass was under way because the play called for the cherry-picker to break down into the deep frontside area known as the Blue. During the Gangster Pass he would be studying the inside linebacker for a cue to cherry-pick or catch the short Red-Dog Pass. So the play had to be specially called in the huddle and bore the tag of Gangster Pass Hardnose. We figured that Frontside Four, continually pestering our frontside end by bumping him and shoving him at the start, was definitely committed to short zone coverage, and that if we could get a man fast into the White area to hold the deep middle defender, then we could swoop down upon Frontside Five with our basketball fast break, two on one, with our man in motion to his outside and our other halfback to his inside.

The play went on long motion with the moving halfback midway between the wingback and the split end before the ball was snapped. At the snap signal the man in motion turned downfield and tore along the sideline at top speed expecting to catch a long high-arched pass over his inside shoulder, a pass thrown about the seventh step after his break.

The other receiver in the two-on-one fast break, the wingback, broke to his favorite cherry-picking spot where he planted himself and pivoted for the inside boundary of Blue Territory. By insisting that he break straight downfield after faking his cherry-pick, we found that he would run the proper course and not get so close to his other halfback that Frontside Five could cover them both.

The quarterback needed seven steps to get the pass away. Therefore, he had plenty of time to let Frontside Five tell him where to throw the football. If he found Frontside Five moving toward the left (Passer's left), he threw to the right, high and far, to the halfback in motion, a pass normally about 35 yards down the sideline. If he found the deep defender moving toward the right, he threw to the left to the cherry-picker breaking into the Blue, a shorter pass 15 to 20 yards beyond the line of scrimmage. Although, because we had no way of letting our stationary halfback in on the

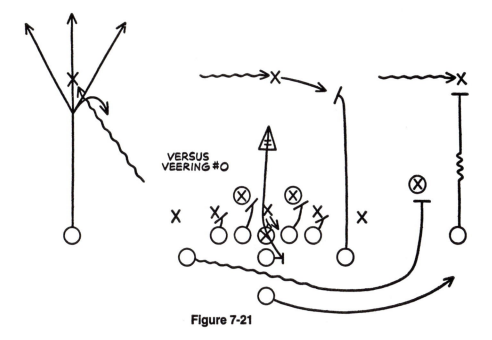

Figure 7-21

scheme, we could not include the Gangster Pass Hardnose among the many automatic possibilities prevalent when operating the Gangster Pass as such, still having called the Hardnose in the huddle we might never get to it because one of the automatic maneuvers popped up:

1. We could throw the Automatic Pass to the backside end regardless of what play in the entire offense had been called (except the punt play).

2. A red-dogging linebacker on his side would cause the wingback to forget the Hardnose Pass and look for the Red-Dog Flip; so would that same linebacker going in motion with our man in motion.

3. A Frontside Four up in Blitz position would make our frontside end forget the Hardnose Pass and look for the Blitz Pass instead.

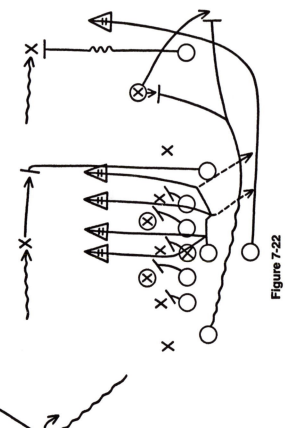

Figure 7-22

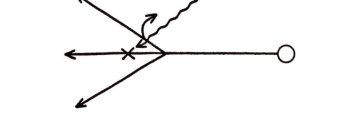

78

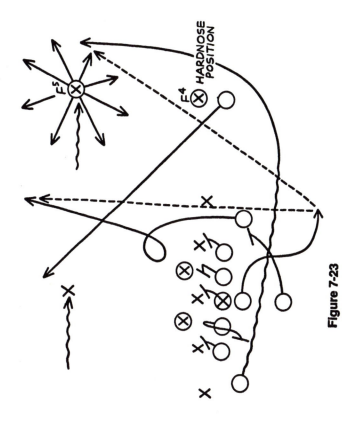

HARDNOSE POSITION

Figure 7-23

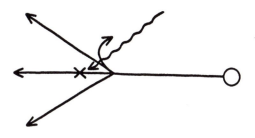

79

4. A Frontside Four dropped off in the Walkaway position would alert our end to disregard the Hardnose call and figure on the Walkaway Pass.

Only if Frontside Four remained in the Hardnose position would the quarterback ever permit the play to develop into the Hardnose pass he had called in the huddle. Although the unsuspecting wingback, still thinking the Hardnose was on, went through with his deep cut, we still had a pretty good Walkaway Pass (Figure 7-24).

In fact if you are a fastidious fellow who considers the cherry-pick block unsportsmanlike, then this is the way for you to work the play. Actually it first appeared in our drawing board this way, except the wingback did not fake the cherry-pick but rushed down upon the safety man and cut according to the Polecat angle rule.

FRONTSIDE FINALE

"Rush the passer," many coaches have said, "for that is the best pass defense of them all." We have no quarrel with that viewpoint. It just might be the gospel truth.

However, our Gangster Pass on the frontside, with its built-in system of automatics for coping with red-dogging linebackers and linebackers in motion and blitzing cornermen, caused us to look down our long skinny noses at defenses that roared in with a lot of noise.

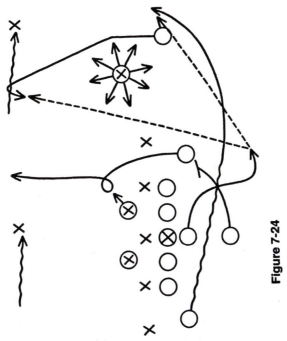

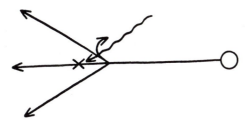

Figure 7-24

Chapter 8

Backside Gangster

We drew up our Run-and-Shoot offense with both ends always split and with a halfback going in motion on every play except the two formal automatics, the Automatic Pass and the Automatic Sneak. We thought that before long we would put in variations by calling one of the ends home and stationing a halfback in regular position and starting some plays without motion. We figured that eventually the defense would key the motion and give us trouble. However, the offense was never stopped. So we never changed. The ease with which we consistently moved the football with a wide-open gambling offense that looked down its long skinny nose and spat at consistency absolutely amazed us. We went the full four years with just the plays described in this book—no more, no less. We discovered that our backside attack away from motion took the starch out of any defense geared toward the motion. The longer motion of the Gangster made this series especially adaptable to a backside attack.

INFLUENCE OF THE POLECAT

You recall that the job of the backside end was always to toy with the man left covering him after whatever adjustment the defense made toward the motion the other way. Almost without fail we could expect a one-on-one situation on the backside. The exception was an occasional dropped-off Backside Three covering the flat. That backside end standing out there all by his lonesome with only one solitary soul assigned to him certainly looked like money in the bank.

Each end was obligated to name his cut in the huddle when the quarterback called the Throwback Pass, our favorite maneuver for hitting away from motion. However, the end's call, though strategic in planning, sometimes turned out tactical in operation: Occasionally in going downfield for his pass cut, the one he had just announced to his quarterback, the backside end found the deep backside defender showing up in a spot other than anticipated. However, we were once again saved by the old Lonesome Polecat, whose receiving rule read:

1. "He right—I left."
2. "He left—I right."
3. "He come—I go."
4. "He go—I stay."

(See "Point of Decision" in Chapter 2.)

The end's quick decision to change the course he had just given the quarterback in the huddle had to be made by his fifth step as he rushed under control downfield toward his defender. On his next couple of steps he had to show the quarterback the direction of his cut, because the trigger man, just completing his own fifth step, now had his eyes glued on the end preparing to send this receiver the football on the next couple steps each man would take (Figure 8-1).

We had great luck on throwback passes when the end took the cut he had announced in the huddle. The close timing of the pass with the receiver's cut made it almost mandatory that the end execute his huddle call. In fact a number of times the first year we were almost at the point of insisting he go through with his announced cut. Such insistence would have been contrary to Polecat philosophy: go reckless, stay loose, and enjoy life. We kept it loose, chiefly because of a number of touchdowns scored spectacularly after the end had bolted into a new course and the quarterback had thrown from a semi-scramble (nine steps). We kept it tactical.

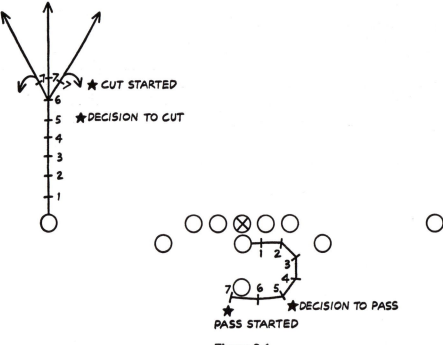

Figure 8-1

So long as the quarterback could start the ball on its way to the target before the end had taken more than a couple of steps along his new course, we were in business. The longer the passer waited after the receiver had committed himself to his new course, the better the chance the defender had of getting under full throttle and covering the pass.

LEANING TOWARD THE TARGET

A right-handed quarterback, passing on the run, right or left, will start the ball backward toward his ear the moment his left foot strikes the ground, and he will begin the snap forward the instant his right foot hits. There must be absolutely no hesitation between the backward and the forward movement of the passing arm. If there is a hesitation, the passer needs to bring the ball forward again, take two more steps, and repeat the throwing action. On all passes longer than ten yards he must start *leaning toward the target* as he starts the ball backward so that he will be planting his right foot downfield the moment he begins the snap forward. His forward momentum will thus enable him to whip the ball 50 yards if necessary. Except occasionally on a scramble he will rarely need that long a pass.

THE THROWBACK PASS

In making the Throwback Pass to the left, the quarterback called in the huddle, "Gangster Pass Right, Throwback" (Figure 8-2).

We wanted all defensive people to absorb thoroughly with their eyes our Hardnose Look on the motion side (Figure 7-23). So, if they had veering linemen and red-dogging linebackers, let those vicious fellows veer and red-dog to their hearts' content to our *motion side*—that was the place where we had been lashing at them all evening. If they had Unwelcome Strangers to pour into Frontside Territory, let them pour—the more, the merrier.

The long motion gave the opposition a chance to make a maximum adjustment to our frontside. Each frontside receiver ran his Hardnose pass-cut except that the wingback cut hard and shallow toward the backside hook area to be available in case of a scramble. Each lineman blocked the same as on any play to the right, run or pass, with one exception: the backside guard or the center, whichever of these two was uncovered, took a more direct course for the backside crasher to cut down this man's penetration so the circling quarterback could have operating space to get his sights set on his backside receiver and his pass away without a scramble if possible.

The quarterback went straight down the line toward the frontside as usual for two steps, took his third step diagonally

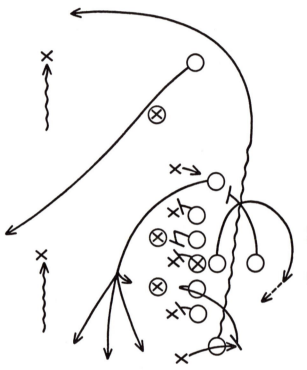

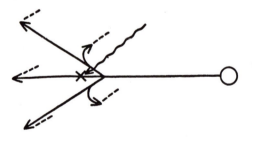

Figure 8-2

backward, all the while giving his halfback in long motion a soul-searching look-off as if he intended passing to him, and then pushed off his left foot on his fourth step to start his reverse course to the backside. With his fifth step he was reading his backside end for the latter's cut against his lone defender. The end running under control was also usually at his fifth step, his point of decision, for normally a running receiver and a running passer are moving step for step. In order to time up our slower quarterbacks with our faster receivers, we had the quarterback learn to run with shorter quicker steps. A football player should run with short, quick steps anyway so long as there is trouble ahead, for he will be under better control for changing direction when his problems ahead shift on him. Obviously, when a ball carrier sees nothing ahead of him but fresh air and sunshine, then he should throw his ears back, step on the high-test, and stride on up the glory road.

STRANDING THE BACKSIDE DEFENDER

Just how much of an angle in or out a backside end took at his point of decision depended on just how much of an angle he found his defender taking at that point (Figure 8-3).

The end's angle rule was: *cut away from your defender at a 90-degree angle.* Thus with the ball thrown on the side of the receiver away from the defender, the latter was forced to run the hypotenuse of a right triangle while the receiver was running one of the shorter arms. We decided earlier in Chapter 5 (Figure 5-2) that the receiver had the advantage. Of course, with a defensive man riding such close herd on a receiver that our boy could practically reach out and touch him, angles were no factor; so during such instances we asked our pass-receiving folks "to throw their ears back, step on the high-test, and beat 'em to the goal line."

With a defender backing off at least five yards straight away from the backside end on the Throwback Pass, our receiver could use his angle rule and cut at 90 degrees straight for either sideline. This probably would have been all right;

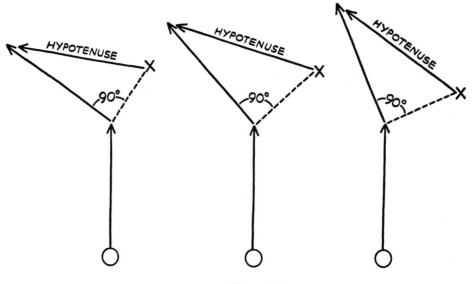

Figure 8-3

however, we decided the simpler thing to do was hook right there. So we explained it to our ends this way: You use your angle rule when at your point of decision your defender assumes an *angle* on your right or left; if he is straight ahead of you, break past him when he is close and hook when he is deep.

The Gangster Throwback Pass was a vital part of our offense. We thank the Lonesome Polecat for the maneuver.

THE COMEBACK PASS

Since a vicious rush consistently by Backside Three cut down on the freedom of our quarterback as he circled for the Throwback Pass, we had to put in something to soften the pressure put on by this backside crasher. One of the answers was the Gangster Comeback Pass (Figure 8-4). As on the Throwback Pass the play went on long motion with the frontside putting on a Hardnose show, except that again the wingback headed for the backside hook area from which

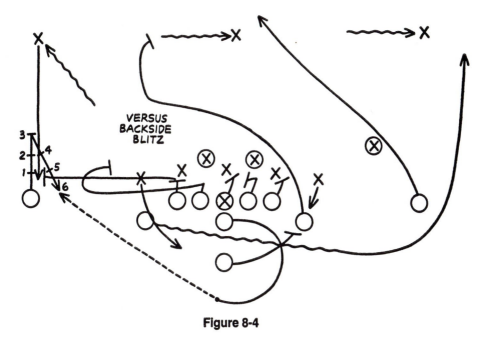

Figure 8-4

he could turn downfield upon Backside Five. The center, the frontside guard, and the frontside tackle all blocked the same as on any play to the motion side. The backside tackle rammed a high hard shoulder (either one) into Backside Two to check his penetration and then ran straight down the line of scrimmage for Backside Four who would come rushing up as the pass was thrown to the backside end. The backside guard used the same procedure on Backside One unless this defender was back off the line. In this case he took a short jab step at him before following the course of his left tackle toward the spot where the receiver was setting himself to catch the pass. About three yards this side of that spot, he turned back toward the inside for the first unfriendly fellow coming out to tackle the pass catcher.

The pass-receiving end took three steps under control toward the deep defender (Backside Four) but with knees thrusting high to simulate top speed. He planted his left foot on his third step and returned toward the passer for three steps, still under control and ready to play first base on a pass coming to him left or right or high or low.

The quarterback started down the line toward the frontside, circled back, and about the time he completed his half-circle, threw the pass as the receiver was still moving toward him. We cannot repeat this too often: that all passes of a hook nature should be executed with the hooking receiver still moving up to the very moment the ball actually leaves the passer's hand. Why? Standing receivers, immediately read by every man and woman and child on the field and in the stands, are at the mercy of nearby interceptors who can get a toehold in the turf and spring on an interception course with the forward movement of the passer's arm. Happily, the running pass is more difficult to intercept because of the lightning-like nature of the throwing action.

The Gangster Comeback pass was built for one person and one person only, Mr. Backside Three when he liked to sell out and blow into the backside of our backfield and grab up all the tickets. Anytime the ornery rascal suddenly changed his tactics by staying home and not crashing, then a Gangster Scramble was on, and the intended receiver broke for depth, picking a course left, right, straight ahead, or hook. We have said that roughly 10 percent of all our plays ended in scrambles.

THE COUNTER PLAY

If on the other hand, Backside Three showed a consistent tendency to back off, to walk away, either at the start of long motion before the ball was snapped or with the snap itself, we liked to hammer at this soft backside with the Counter Play, which could be a run or a pass depending on what Backside Three did (Figure 8-5). When the quarterback's call was "Gangster Right, Counter," the man in motion and the right end ran their Hardnose courses to the frontside, but the right wingback again cut as shallow and as fast as he could for the backside hook area. The blocking linemen and

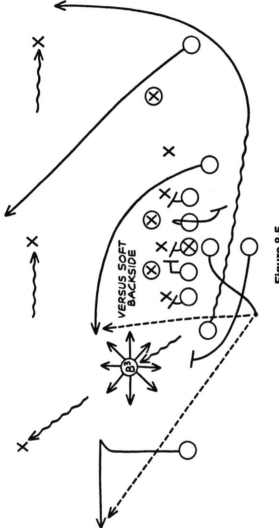

VERSUS SOFT BACKSIDE

Figure 8-5

91

the fullback accepted the word "counter" as meaning "opposite," and they obligingly blocked to the left, the linemen using a hard right shoulder and the fullback resorting to his favorite block on Backside Three: "Break the far leg with your inside shoulder, drop to all fours as you turn your body downfield, dig him for five yards, and make him escape to the backside." As we stated earlier, the fullback's block, used by all our players in the open field and executed at half-speed during our pre-practice and pre-game warm-up drills, boiled itself down during actual game conditions to the first coaching point, the hard overthrow at the far leg.

The left end took four steps straight downfield, again under control but simulating full speed by running with knees high. He planted his inside foot on his fourth step and cut straight for the sideline.

The passer coming left along the line two steps, started the ball back toward his ear as his left foot hit the ground on his diagonal step backward (third step) and snapped it toward the receiver as his right foot hit the ground on his fourth step. The passer permitted Backside Three to tell him where to throw the football:

1. "He left—I right."
2. "He right—I left."
3. "He up—I back."
4. "He back—I run."

If the quarterback, as he came down the line, found Frontside Three moving left in his Walkaway position, the ball was passed toward the right to the wingback coming across toward the hook zone. If the trigger man found the defender moving toward the right in his backed-off spot, the pass was made to the left to the split end just as the receiver was pushing off his inside foot for the sideline. If Frontside Three was found coming back up to contain the running passer, the throw was made to either receiver, but we preferred the sideline because "Mr. Sideline never intercepts a pass." If the quarterback as he came down the line found

Frontside Three still backing off, he yelled, "Go," which was a signal for the fullback to turn down upon Backside Three and the left end to turn down on Backside Four (Figure 8-6). The right wingback, coming across looking for a pass but hearing the go signal instead, turned down for Backside Five. It mattered not to the linemen that the pass had turned into a run, because they always blocked the same way, run or pass.

COUNTER PASS DELAYED

At first, in working the Gangster Counter Play, we took it for granted that the defensive halfback assigned to our backside end would show respect for our receiver by staying back on the short counter pass. This was normally the case. However, there came a night against a drop-off Backside Three when we hit the end so often on this short sideline pass that the deep defender decided to come up and stick his nose in. Naturally our quarterback started a scramble, a scramble that scored a touchdown in the last quarter and put us ahead in a game that would have won us the state championship had we not permitted the following kick-off to return all the way.

The scramble on the Gangster Counter Play that scored the touchdown so handily we put in as a regular option (Figure 8-7). We referred to the maneuver as Gangster Counter Pass Delayed. When the quarterback, as he cocked his arm for the short sideline pass to his backside end, saw the deep defender up in the receiver's hair, he returned the ball to its forward position in front of his chest, scrambled toward the sideline, and lofted the pass in a high arch about 25 yards down the sideline.

The instant the receiver saw the scrambling action of the quarterback, he did not as during the usual scramble look downfield and establish a point of decision before making a new cut—he *knew* what his cut should be; he *knew* the halfback was in his hair; so he lit out for the flag, looking for the ball over his inside shoulder.

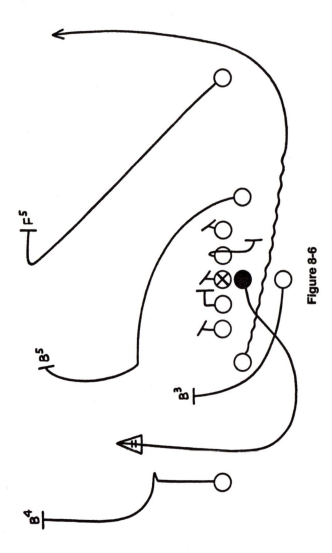

Figure 8-6

94

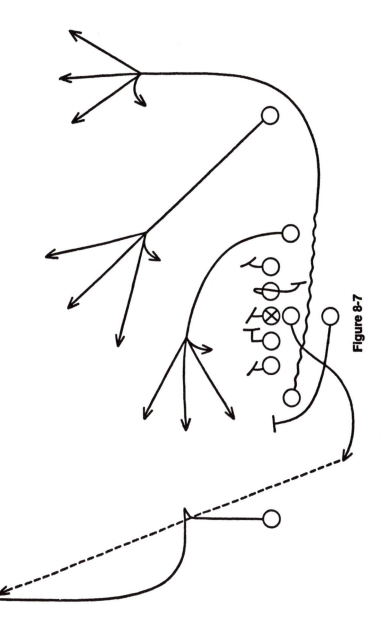

Figure 8-7

95

All other receivers, seeing that a scramble was on, did what they normally did on any scramble: each took a quick look at the defender in his area and established a new cut.

If the quarterback had circled back to the frontside, a typical Gangster scramble would have been under way (Figure 8-8). You recall that the wingback always scrambled to the side toward which the quarterback himself was scrambling. On any scramble, after their initial blocks, the five blocking linemen and the fullback got to their feet and rushed Polecat fashion down the line whichever way the quarterback had gone. But the linemen were careful not to cross the line of scrimmage until they were sure the quarterback had tucked the ball away for keeps.

POINTS OF EMPHASIS

We would like to emphasize the following points concerning the Backside Gangster:

1. We disciplined ourselves to hit away from motion one play out of every four, oftener than that when we faced consistently overshifted defenses.

2. Our favorite backside play was the Throwback Pass.

3. Against a hard rushing backside end we occasionally used the Comeback Pass.

4. Against a soft backside in which the defensive end dropped off, we liked the Counter Play.

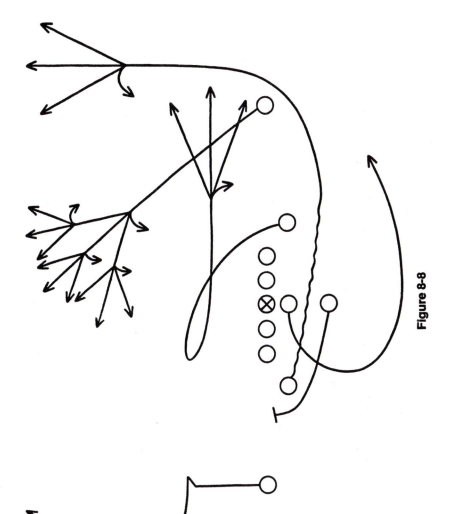

Figure 8-8

Chapter 9

The Cowboy Series

We scored more touchdowns and gained more yardage and got into more scrambles and brought the fans more times screaming to their feet and had *more interceptions* with the Cowboy Series than with any other pattern of play in our repertoire. We loved the Cowboy. Next to the Gangster, the Cowboy was our favorite.

Where the Gangster Series was basically a fast-striking weapon, the Cowboy plays were more delayed. Where the Gangster had the quarterback passing on his third, fifth, or seventh step to the right and his fourth, sixth, or eighth step to the left, the Cowboy asked him to pass on his ninth step to the right and his tenth to the left. Anything more than eight steps put the Gangster into a scramble while it took eleven steps before the Cowboy went scrambling.

COWBOY ON THE RUN

The Cowboy Run was a three-way option (Figure 9-1). Like all Cowboy plays this run, Cowboy Run Right, started on short motion with the ball being snapped the instant the left halfback arrived two yards behind his left tackle. The quarterback stepped down the line with his first three steps exactly the same as on the Gangster Series but with his eyes glued on Frontside Three all the way. You recall that we expected one man on the defense to tell us what to do. Frontside Three would by his actions determine whether we worked the first option or the second.

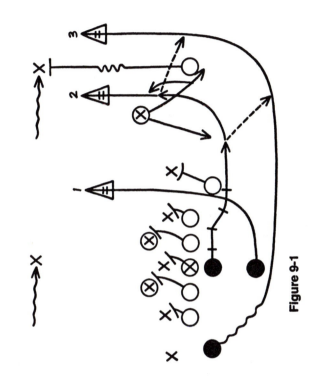
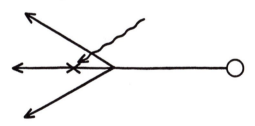

Figure 9-1

On his diagonal step backward the quarterback, looking squarely at Frontside Three, saw his fullback from the corner of his eye and placed the football under his teammate's chin-high left elbow, riding it upon the man's stomach until it had traveled from in front of his own right hip to his left hip. The belly ride took place while the quarterback was executing a short fourth step straight toward the sideline but behind the fullback so as not to trip him. During these four steps plus the ones that followed there absolutely was no slowing down in the quarterback's movements—the trigger man was *running*. The ride started when his right foot hit the ground on his third step and ended when his left foot hit on his fourth step. If, during the ride he found Frontside Three fighting to the outside of our wingback's head-on spear block, he let the fullback keep the ball. He signaled the ball carrier by ramming the ball upward on the fullback's stomach toward his chest. Feeling the ball being jerked upward, the fullback clamped it with both forearms and drove straight ahead inside Frontside Three. The fullback, who had also been watching Frontside Three all the way, had a premonition he would be permitted to keep the ball when he saw his defender fighting to the outside.

On the other hand if Frontside Three was fighting to the inside of our wingback's block, the quarterback took the ball away from the fullback and headed straight for the sideline toward Frontside Four, while the fullback drove like a madman across the line of scrimmage just *outside* Frontside Three—outside, because the hole was there for him to roar through clean and attract the attention of linebackers and secondary. Now we would let Frontside Four tell us what to do with the football. If Frontside Four challenged our quarterback, the trigger man made a one-handed flip pass at a 45 degree angle backward to the left halfback. At the snap signal this halfback had sped through a point one yard behind where a normal right halfback would line up in a full-house backfield and then straightened out toward the sideline looking for the quarterback's pitch. He did not turn downfield until the ball was pitched or the quarterback himself turned downfield.

If Frontside Four instead of challenging our quarterback stayed out to cover the wide-running left halfback, the signal caller kept the ball and leveled off straight upfield. If the quarterback saw Frontside Four leaving the halfback when he leveled off, then just before getting tackled the trigger man made his flip pass to the halfback, who had turned downfield with the quarterback but well outside the ball handler.

MOVEMENT OF THE FULLBACK

In executing the Cowboy Run right, the fullback, always in a parallel, three-point stance, pushed with his left foot straight toward the sideline as he had done in going for Frontside Three on Gangster passes. Then he headed for the ride area by rounding off his course and aiming for a spot one yard behind his right tackle. Eyes fastened on Frontside Three, he ran with his left elbow chin-high and his right hand palm up below his belt so that the quarterback from the corner of his eye had a big pocket in which to place the ball for its ride. The moment the fullback felt the ball on his stomach, he lowered his left arm and raised his right, but he did not clamp the ball tightly unless he felt the upward, ramming action toward his chest. Feeling such a movement, he tightened his grip and drove inside Frontside Three while the quarterback and the left halfback faked toward the sideline at top speed for ten yards. During his ten-yard dash toward the sideline the quarterback looked intently at Frontside Four to get his attention and hold him away a second from the play inside.

BLOCKING FOR THE COWBOY RUN

The frontside end ran under control straight downfield toward Frontside Five exactly as on Gangster Run, stalked his prey until the defender took a step forward, and then threw an open field block into his lap. The backside end as usual on all plays to the frontside toyed with his deep defender setting him up for a throwback pass later. The linemen blocked as they did on any play to the right, run or pass.

The spear block employed by the right halfback, we got from Woody Hayes years ago at Ohio State University. The blocker aimed his eyeballs at the defender's jersey number and drove his forehead into this spot, taking the man right or left whichever way he wanted to go. This block, generously employed by possession coaches, but often called brutal by sportswriters, is anything but brutal. Through lack of understanding, some of the typewriter athletes have described a gruesome picture of the blocker under a full head of steam roaring into a poor helpless defensive man as if a steel knife protruded from the top of his lowered head. The block is not brutal. Its greatest attribute is its capacity for leeching onto a defensive lineman and staying with him until he commits himself right or left. We considered Woody's block as absolutely indispensable in handling Frontside Three on our Cowboy Run.

There were nights when the Cowboy Run was our best gainer on the ground. Anytime we found our quarterback turning the corner with the football outside Frontside Three, we felt our hair roots tingle and our belly muscles harden because we were now in business and operating at full capacity. The Cowboy would howl tonight!

However, we needed to give the ball to the fullback often enough to keep Frontside Three respecting him and fighting inside our wingback's spear block.

THE COWBOY PASS

If our fullback on the Cowboy Run could hurt the opposition enough inside Frontside Three, then we had a great pass cooking (Figure 9-2). In working Cowboy Pass Right, each end rushed straight downfield toward his deep defender, using the rule established by the Lonesome Polecat, which required a deep receiver by his fifth step to have his mind made up on his cut so that within the next couple of

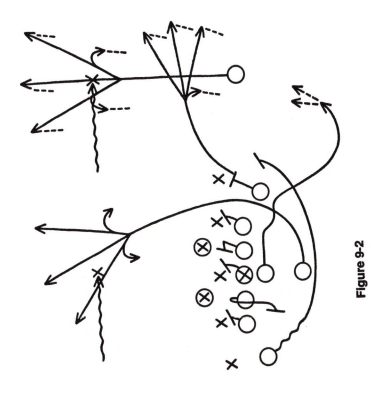

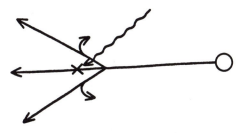

Figure 9-2

103

steps he would break right or left at an angle of 90 degrees away from a defender playing to one side of him, or rush on straight through a defender playing him head-on and close, or hook right there on the spot if he found the defender backed off straight away five yards or more.

The right wingback bumped Frontside Three to simulate his assignment on the Cowboy Run, so that he could not be used as a key by a deep defender to tip off "pass." After the bump block, made with whichever shoulder was convenient, he hastened into the right flat (Polecat Heaven). The fullback, if he did not get tackled—for we still insisted that he make a good fake—broke down the middle upon the safety man.

The right end and the right halfback were the chief receivers on the Cowboy Pass Right. After calling the snap number the quarterback ran down the line looking for the position of Frontside Four. Only the Blitz position worried him. If he found the corner man in the Walkaway or the Hardnose position (Figures 7-1, 7-2, 7-3), he expected smooth sailing. After completing the ride to the fullback he shoved away from his lateral fourth step straight backward with his fifth to start getting depth for his pass. On his sixth step he started rounding off toward the sideline looking downfield for his right end. He expected normally to throw on his ninth step; therefore, he had a few steps to read his deep receiver who would start his getaway along about his seventh step. Broken down, the right end's moves were as follows:

1. Looking in at the ball, he got off with the snap.
2. For five steps straight downfield he studied his deep defender and selected his cut.
3. On his sixth or seventh step, depending on whether he was cutting right or left, he broke 90 degrees away from the defensive halfback unless this defender was head-on.
4. If he found the man head-on and close, he challenged him to a foot race to the goal line.

5. If he found him head-on but five yards or more away, he collected up and turned for a hook pass.

Our quarterback always ran under control until a scramble was on. The receivers were also moving under control until the moment they made their final cuts. There was no reason why controlled running could not be coordinated to the point where both passer and receiver moved practically step for step (Figure 9-3).

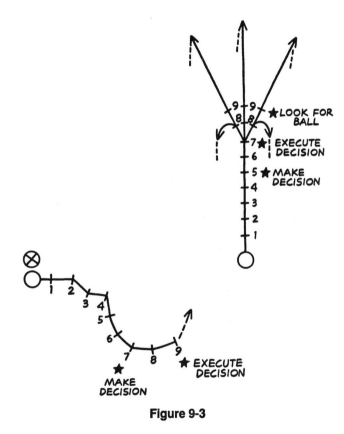

Figure 9-3

We found that the longer passes required the quarterback to step downfield with his right foot before starting the ball forward on its release, because the downfield movement of the body gave momentum to the pass. To accomplish this downfield step with his right foot, it was necessary for him to start leaning toward the target the moment his left foot hit the ground on the preceding step (Figure 9-4). On running passes to the right, this lean toward the target brought the right foot across the left in a cross-over step. On running passes to the left, the lean caused a push-off from the left foot as the right foot open-stepped downfield. Some of our quarterbacks, even though right-handed, actually preferred throwing to the left than to the right. Evidently it is easier to open up than to cross over.

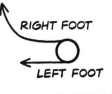

FOOTWORK OF
RIGHT-HANDED
PASSER THROWING
WHILE RUNNING
TO HIS RIGHT

FOOTWORK OF
SAME PASSER
WHILE RUNNING
TO HIS LEFT

Figure 9-4

COWBOY PASS BLITZ

If during his first two steps down the line the quarterback found Frontside Four crashing across from the Blitz position on a course designed to cut off his lateral progress toward his ninth step, he whipped the ball to the frontside end on his third step exactly as he had done on Gangster Pass Blitz (Figure 9-5). Obviously he made no fake to the fullback—there was not time. The receiver took his cue from the Blitz position of Frontside Four and cut inside on his third step at a 30-degree angle. Only these two men knew the Blitz Pass was in operation. The other nine offensive men performed the duties assigned on Cowboy Pass Right.

A quarterback who ignored Frontside Four crashing from the Blitz position soon became a Christian after getting nailed to the cross a few times as he tried to level off about his

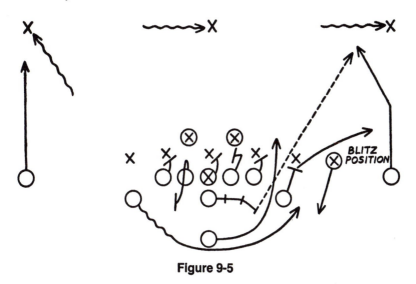

Figure 9-5

sixth step. Still some of our more mobile trigger men could scramble and dump the ball into the flat (into Heaven) to the right halfback while catching a flying Frontside Four in their laps. A quarterback like that will make you a great coach— you will end the season ten pounds fatter than you started (Figure 9-6). Notice that, when he saw the quarterback scrambling, the right end, having played his cue and cut in on his third step for the Blitz Pass, now planted his left foot on his sixth step and struck out toward his defender on a scramble course.

COWBOY PASS OPTION

Even though on the Cowboy Pass we were sending the fullback through to swoop down on the safety man, we did not want him to make a poor fake in order not to get tackled at the line of scrimmage. Far from it—we wanted the best fake in the world; we wanted Frontside Three to tackle him, because then we were really in business. Then, we had on the coals another version of the Cowboy Option Play (Figure 9-7).

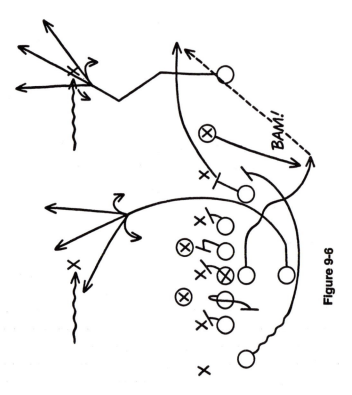

Figure 9-6

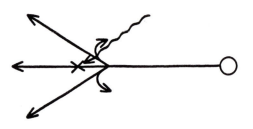

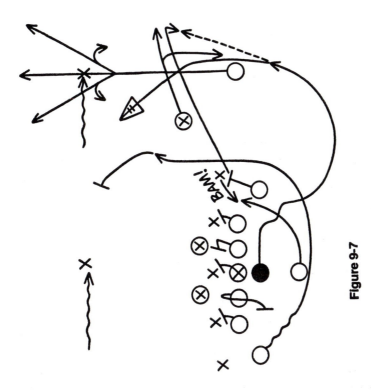

Figure 9-7

On this play the quarterback ordered in the huddle
Cowboy Pass Right. Our fullback made his usual fine fake
and got tackled by Frontside Three. The left halfback, without even slowing down when he found no crasher outside
the ride area, cut straight downfield looking for a pass over
his outside shoulder. The quarterback rolling to the outside
found nothing but fresh air and sunshine to roll into. Great!
He kept rolling, still holding the ball in both hands in front
of his chest. To all receivers a scramble was on. But this was
better than a scramble—this was something definite, specific,
surefire. The wingback's job on a scramble was to break to
the flat toward which the quarterback was rolling—but he
was already in this particular flat. Now the option began. If,
as the quarterback approached the line of scrimmage on the
dead run, scramble fashion, Frontside Four left the halfback
in the flat and came up to stop the quarterback's run, the
trigger man pushed a simple one-handed lob to the halfback
standing along the sideline. If Frontside Four stayed back to
guard the flat, the quarterback tucked the ball away at the
line of scrimmage and roared on into the night.

It was the Cowboy Option except that the quarterback
made his pitch forward instead of backward, every bit as
good and maybe even a little better because now the halfback
had seven or eight yards gained the instant he caught the
pitch, and if he dropped it the opponents could not recover
it as on the regular option play. So, our fullback always made
a great fake as he bolted into the line on the Cowboy Series.
Whereas on the Gangster Series we had needed a fullback
who absolutely loved to hit people, now on the Cowboy we
required one who loved to fake like a maniac.

COWBOY BACKSIDE ATTACK

The Throwback Pass from the Cowboy Series was almost identical to that from the Gangster except for Cowboy
ball handling (Figure 9-8). The wingback came across shallow and fast to help out in case a scramble developed. As on
the Gangster Throwback the quarterback normally prepared

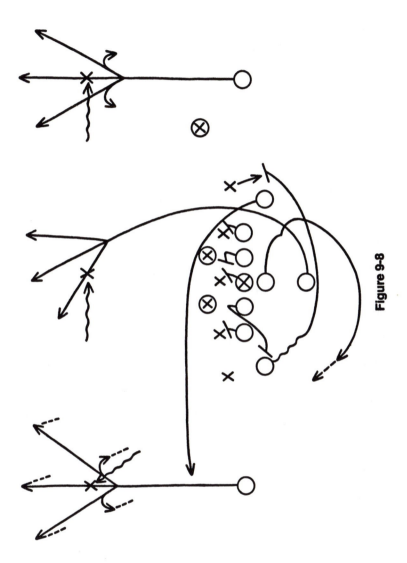

Figure 9-8

111

himself to get his pass away on his seventh step, but if he had enough room to take nine steps, he usually took them. After that, a scramble was on.

By now the course of the receivers during a scramble certainly must have been evident. All they did was hastily reappraise the position of their defenders and make new cuts each in his own area, so that the quarterback could always depend on a receiver in each of three areas (Red, White, and Blue) making an intelligent effort to free himself for the Scramble Pass. The passer also knew as he scrambled toward the line of scrimmage in the flat areas (Heaven and Hell) that the halfback who had not gone in motion would be there readying himself for a short pass.

BLOCK OF THE COWBOY HALFBACK

On all Cowboy passes the halfback in motion used the same block on Frontside Three that the fullback threw against the fellow during Gangster passes. The blocking halfback started out on the same course he would have taken on the Cowboy Run except that instead of running through a point one yard deeper than the spot where the other halfback would have lined up in a fullhouse backfield, he now went right through this spot. He practically brushed the quarterback stepping backward after his ride to the fullback. Here is a vital coaching point: halfbacks will show a tendency to slow down and wait for Frontside Three to come to them. Such delay will foul up the play. Number one, it looks like a pass block and tips off the defense. Number two, it hinders the quarterback's movements and restricts his vision. Number three, it is contrary to Run-and-Shoot philosophy, which features *motion*—human bodies in motion around a ball in motion—because *motion* on the field creates *emotion* in the stands.

Chapter 10

The Wagon Train Series

The Wagon Train appeared third on our daily work program next to the Gangster and the Cowboy. The series provided our attack with a sudden change of pace around end, a fast burst by the man in motion. It was more muscular than the first two series; yet it had its deception. It was an old-fashioned guard-pulling arrangement adapted to the Run-and-Shoot philosophy.

WAGON TRAIN EAST OR WEST

The Wagon Train sweep vied with the Cowboy Run for the best average among our running plays (Figure 10–1). We called the sweep to the right Wagon Train East and the one to the left Wagon Train West, because on a map east is to the right and west is to the left. This play belonged to our Clutch Series, which was a small group of plays we sometimes worked without going into a huddle, to hold back the clock just before the half or the end of the game. When we were in such a clutch and the quarterback wanted the sweep from the Wagon Train, he stepped to the ball and bellowed, "Wagon Train East!" (or West) so that all could hear.

Using East and West for this clutch play instead of Right and Left even when calling it in the huddle, cut down on some of the thinking when we were in a bind with the timer's clock running out.

113

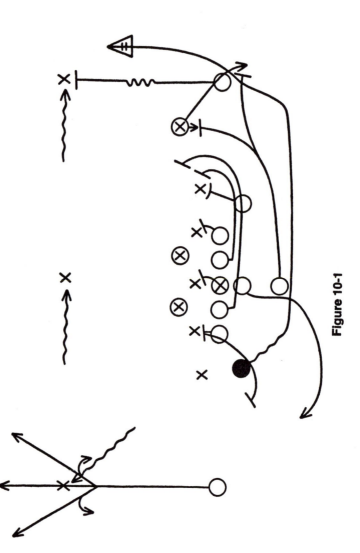

Figure 10-1

In working Wagon Train East the right end went downfield the way he did on all plays to his side, stalked the deep defender as if he were keying him for a pass cut, and threw a block into him the moment he started forward. The left end as usual toyed with his defensive man and studied him for a backside pass. The right wingback used a Woody Hayes' spear block (already explained in Chapter 9) on Frontside Three, trying to keep him stalemated on the line until the right guard pulled around and sealed him off from the ball carrier.

The right tackle drove into Frontside Two with his usual left-shoulder drive, while the center did the same on Number Zero. The left guard pulled around the horn and sealed off the inside against the first linebacker coming out from the middle. The left tackle took a jab step with his inside foot into Backside Two, circled backward and outward for an overthrow on Backside Three. The fullback rushed laterally for Frontside Four, using the block he had employed so often on Frontside Three (Chapter 7) while working Gangster passes. However, there was this difference: if Frontside Four rushed across the line of scrimmage and got penetration, the fullback, though still aiming his left shoulder at the outside leg knee-high, found it impossible to turn downfield after throwing his body; so he now rode around into a reverse body block with his head toward his own goal line.

The ball carrier away on short motion took the ball on the dead run under his chin-high inside elbow and following close upon the fullback went wide or cut back according to the fullback's block.

The quarterback starting from his parallel stance in which he had kept most of his weight on his right foot to prevent a false step forward, whirled straight backward with his left foot toward the fullback's position and handed off the ball on his second step. The moment his left foot hit the ground on his third step he pushed for the backside and rounded off behind his left tackle, who shielded him from Backside Three in case that lad was a "butcher boy," an appropriate term we applied to backside ends coached to "kill the quarterback while he's faking and we'll destroy their offense!"

I sometimes suspect that pro quarterbacks, who really are the greatest football players in the world, sometimes make poor fakes after handing off the football because they do not wish to get clobbered by tons of professional muscle. In fact, many of them peek at the leather lugger after giving him the ball as if to say, "Don't hit me—I gave it to *him!*" We jumped up and down on our caps and insisted that our quarterbacks carry out their fakes. However, we protected our boy on the Wagon Train Series by giving him a personal blocker.

TWO PLAYS IN ONE

But protecting our trigger man was just one of three reasons we dropped the backside tackle to run interference for our faking quarterback on the Wagon Train Sweep. A second reason was that the maneuver gave us a natural automatic. Even though Wagon Train East had been called in the huddle (or yelled at the line of scrimmage during a clutch), the quarterback at his own discretion could fake the ball to the left halfback and roll out behind his left tackle for a throwback pass to the backside end. Also, if the signal caller came away from center without a good handle on the ball and found himself a bit late to hand off to his flying halfback, he still had the throwback pass to fall back on (Figure 10–2). Remember we planned to hit the backside once in every four plays. Recall also that the backside end on all plays to the frontside *always* ran a pass cut against his deep defender, using his Polecat angle-rule. But with only the quarterback and the left halfback knowing that the play was now the Wagon Train Throwback Pass, all other hands deployed themselves for the sweep.

We found in studying the play on the drawing board that we had three problems. The left end was no problem be-

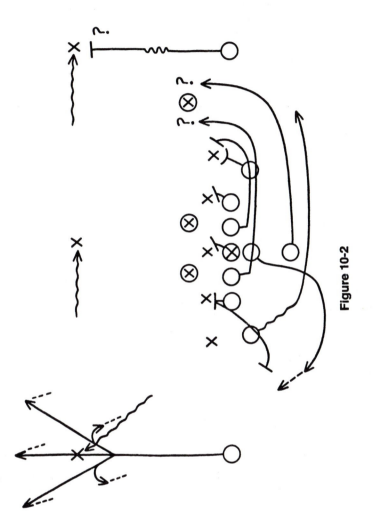

Figure 10-2

117

cause he expected a throwback pass on every play. The left tackle was no problem, for he jabbed at Backside Two and dropped on Backside Three on every Wagon Train play away from him. The center and the right tackle were no problem—they always blocked the same way, run or pass. The right guard and the right wingback were no problem, as their two-timing operation on Frontside Three was at the line of scrimmage and was perfectly legal on a pass play. That left three problems:

1. Would the left guard drive outside the two-on-one block and get caught illegally downfield before the pass was thrown?
2. Would the fullback turn downfield and clobber Frontside Four before the pass was made?
3. Would the right end charge down upon Frontside Five and flatten him while the quarterback was still running out to throw the ball?

To ensure the legality of our Wagon Train Throwback Pass, when it was thrown automatically, we arrived at the following coaching points:

1. The left halfback, the instant the ball was taken away from beneath his raised elbow, brought his right hand to his stomach with his right elbow tight against his side and headed straight for the sideline bellowing like a berserk bull. As he ran he looked intently at Frontside Four. We have already declared that a wide-faking backfield man must glue a meaningful look upon the corner man if the fake is to be worth its salt. Although some of our halfbacks were not very bull-like in their baritones, the mad dash for the sideline plus the meaningful look tended to draw not only Frontside Four on a pursuit course but also the interior linebackers and the frontside linemen.

2. The left guard and the fullback, running not far ahead of the left halfback, heard the bellowing of the bull and themselves struck straight for the sideline (Figure 10–3).

There was still the problem of the right end throwing a block too soon upon Frontside Five. Actually this turned out to be no problem at all for the end normally found himself working on a very cautious fellow, a man who at halftime said to his coach, "How do you tell whether they are going to run or pass?" We found the end throwing his downfield blocks on about his ninth or tenth step and the quarterback passing the Wagon Train Throwback normally on his eighth step; so, we had no problem.

SPLITTING THE DEFENSE'S VISION

A third reason for pulling the backside tackle to run interference for the faking quarterback on the Wagon Train Sweep was to influence the defensive secondary from getting on their pursuit courses the moment the flow started in our backfield. For the flow was split—part of the movement was one way, but the other part, just the opposite (Figure 10–4). Here were the problems the Wagon Train gave the secondary:

1. *Halfbacks:* Is this end coming down to catch a pass or to block me? He always comes down under control glaring at me on every play. If I play inside, he cuts outside. If I play outside, he cuts inside. If I play back, he hooks. If I play up, he breaks past me. And sometimes I end up holding him in my lap.

2. *Safety man:* If I key those pulling guards and rush up to help stop the sweep, I give their backside end two-thirds of the field in which to outmaneuver our halfback when they throw that

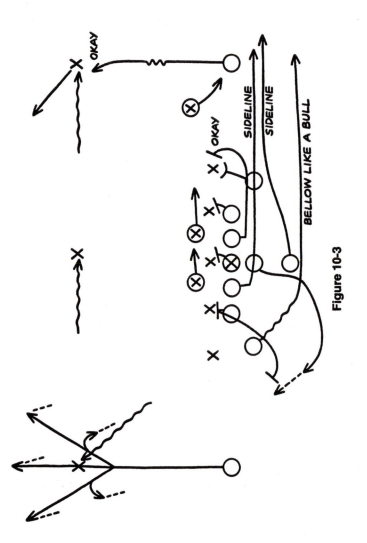

Figure 10-3

120

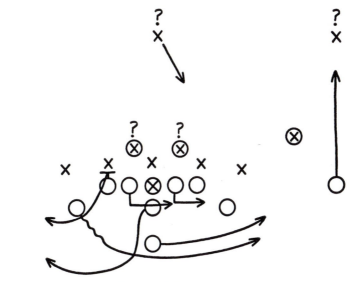

Figure 10-4

backside pass. And they throw passes on any down anywhere on the field. If I just stand here, they'll be operating with eleven men against our ten on that sweep.

3. *Linebackers* (one to the other): Go with the pulling guards if they come your way, and drop off to the backside if they go away from you. We cannot gang up on the same side.

If we called the Wagon Train Throwback Pass in the huddle (for instance, Wagon Train East, Throwback West), we picked up a good second-choice receiver (Figure 10–5). The wingback, instead of spearing Frontside Three as on the sweep, released shallow for the backside hook area. Here he caught many short passes against a backside linebacker who failed to drop off to the backside. The fullback cut up inside the pulling right guard's block on Frontside Three and broke down the middle to give us a good setup in case of a scramble.

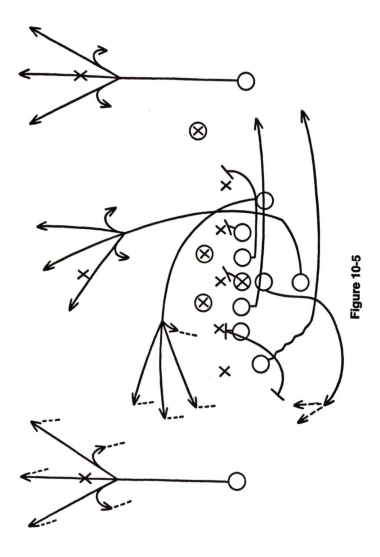

Figure 10-5

122

REVERSING THE WAGON TRAIN

We threw the Wagon Train Sweep into reverse with a play called Wagon Train Reverse; for instance, "Wagon Train East, Reverse West" (Figure 10–6). Both tackles and the center used right shoulders to drive their men. Each guard took two short steps to the right, whirled back to the left behind the quarterback's overthrow block on Backside Three, and sealed things off to the inside. The fullback went hard as ever into his overthrow on Frontside Three.

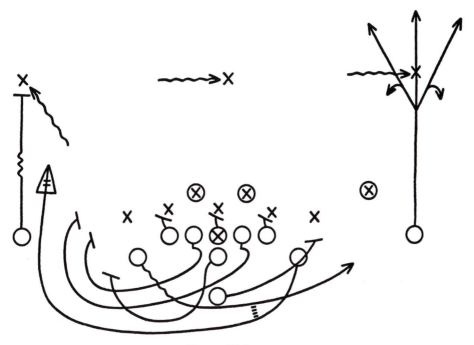

Figure 10-6

The backside end, who became frontside at the word "reverse," performed his usual stalking action on the deep defender on his side, while the frontside end, now backside, ran his toying operation on his man.

The quarterback handed off to the left halfback who took the ball as he ran through the fullback spot and relayed it to the right wingback coming around toward a point one yard behind where the fullback had lined up. The right halfback with no delay had gotten depth by stepping straight back with his left foot at the snap of the ball.

Whenever the guards before the snap found themselves covered head on, as in the four-three defense, they jab-stepped with their right feet into the men over them and pulled back around the horn without using the whirl to get them started (Figure 10–7).

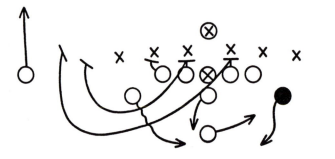

Figure 10-7

INSIDE MUSCLE WANTED

The Gangster, the Cowboy, and the Wagon Train gave us plenty of passing everywhere, but most of the running was outside. If we had stopped with just these three series, we would have faced double-coverage on our split ends every time we set ourselves for a play. The next two chapters will provide the Run-and-Shoot offense with inside muscle.

Chapter 11

The Popcorn Series

The greatest mousetrap play in T formation football has been the fullback trap popularized by Paul Brown and his Cleveland Browns when Marion Motley was the most heralded fullback in the pro game. Running a T offense without the fullback trap would be like running your automobile with a spark plug missing—the thing would sputter and cough and wheeze.

POPCORN TRAP

The fullback trap was the foundation stone in establishing our Popcorn Series (Figure 11-1). We had to be getting solidly into the opposition with good yardage on this trap before we would hurl other Popcorn maneuvers at them.

The Popcorn trap was the only play in our offense which necessitated rule blocking. There was nothing new for the ends, however. Each end at his point of decision (five steps) studied his defender with exactly the same demeanor he normally used in approaching the fellow and threw his usual block the instant the man checked his backward course and started for the fullback. The center's rule on Popcorn Trap Right was "Drive back or post." Those four words he had to memorize off the field until they popped into his head every time he heard "Popcorn Trap." On the field he learned what they meant. "Drive back" meant for him to

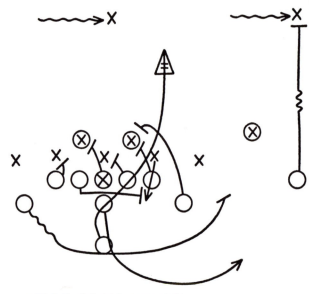

VERSUS AN ODD DEFENSE

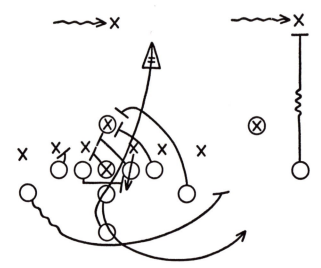

VERSUS AN EVEN DEFENSE

Figure 11-1

drive back upon anybody lined up in front of our left guard. If there was nobody over that guard, then he posted (spearblocked) the man over himself to set him up for the right guard.

The right guard's rule was "Drive back," which ordered him to drive upon anybody lined up over our center; if there was nobody over center, he drove through that spot anyway for the first unfriendly jersey that showed on the backside. The right tackle's rule was "Throw back," which meant for him to throw his body across in front of the first linebacker to his inside to prevent forward penetration and hook him with his outside leg to prevent lateral sliding.

The wingback's rule was also "Throw back." He turned inward after crossing the line and threw his body knee-high at the legs of the linebacker being blocked by the right tackle. This was the same linebacker he had been keying on Gangster passes. This was the gentleman he cherry-picked when he found him staying home on Gangster Pass Walkaway. This was the fellow against whom he caught short passes when he found him red-dogging or going in motion with our halfback in motion.

We found opposing linebackers to be clever, vicious fellows, hard to deal with at best. They were contact kids who loved to play football. They made 75 percent of their team's tackles. Their greatest ambition was to mess up a man's offense. We did not like them, so we plotted all manner of evil against them. That was the reason on Popcorn Trap Right our right halfback doubled up with our right tackle on the near linebacker. Even though the wingback's block was sometimes a clip, it was legal because it was performed in the legal clip zone, an area roughly three yards deep from tackle to tackle.

However, putting our halfback on the linebacker with our tackle prevented our sending a blocker downfield for the safety man. We hoped with the wide spread we had created in the deep secondary that our ball carrier would outmaneuver this tackler. We told our fullback what we announced with pounding fist to all our backfield men: "A great ball carrier will always get rid of the first tackler!" Anyway, we refused to give up our double-team on the linebacker. Incidentally the pounding fist in the palm and the jumping up and down on the cap mentioned earlier are dramatic techniques used in Run-and-Shoot football to emphasize important coaching points, and they prove themselves just as valuable as in power football.

The left guard had a rule short and sweet, "Trap." In his drills on the field he found himself trapping the first penetrator beyond the ball. The left tackle's key word was "Overthrow," in the execution of which he "broke" the inside leg of Backside Two knee-high, hooked his outside leg, turned straight downfield, and dug him for five yards—the standard overthrow block used by our fullback and halfbacks on passes and by the entire team in the open field.

The halfback in motion went into high gear at the snap signal and threw an overthrow block on Frontside Three. The fast move by this halfback was necessary not only to draw Frontside Three across and withhold him from making a downfield tackle on the fullback but also to condition him for the pass play to follow.

The quarterback opened to the backside and ran straight backward toward the fullback's position, placing the ball upon the fullback's stomach beneath the chin-high right elbow. The ball was handed off on the run with the same controlled speed the quarterback always used on every play. After making the hand-off the trigger man rolled to the frontside, holding both hands on his right hip and looking intently at Frontside Four—hands on hip as if he still had the football, and looking at him as if he were studying him for a pass cue. This faking of the quarterback is one of the most important fundamentals in T formation football, yet undoubtedly the most neglected on all levels of coaching. The sadistic head coach who roars, "To hell with the fancy stuff—let's get on with the head-knocking!" needs two things badly: number one, somebody to beat the tar out of him, and number two, somebody to coach his quarterback.

The fullback started with a short step, actually a half-step, with his left foot straight toward the outside foot of his left guard and followed with a full step with his other foot toward the inside foot of this guard. With both the fullback and the quarterback meeting each other on the run, the ball was handed off just as the fullback's inside foot was hitting the ground on the second step and the quarterback's inside foot was halfway through his second step—actually, a step and a half for each man, since the fullback's first step was only a half-step. The fullback's third step was a straight-ahead plant from which he veered toward the daylight wherever it showed.

Having these two men meet on the run served three important purposes:

1. It gave us *movement* throughout the entire team in accordance with the Run-and-Shoot philosophy of motion-motion-everywhere.

2. The backward moving quarterback cleared the way for the fullback to cut sharper to the frontside after taking the hand-off whenever he found the hole clogged by an inside veering lineman (Figure 11-2). A stagnant quarterback—one who takes one

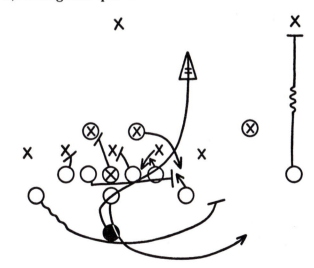

Figure 11-2

step and waits for the fullback to come and get it—
might as well tell the linebackers beforehand he is
going to work the trap play because those crafty
fellows will read the maneuver like a book.

3. A final reason for insisting that the quarterback
   and the fullback pass each other on the run was
   that it set up the Popcorn Pass.

POPCORN PASS

On nights when we were running the trap play effectively, we liked to throw the Popcorn Pass (Figure 11-3).

Each end used his Polecat angle-rule on his defensive
halfback, while the wingback drove hard into the deep middle. The linemen blocked the same as usual unless the
linebackers were playing soft, in which case the backside
guard or the center, whichever was uncovered, jabbed at the
linebacker and dropped for the backside crasher. The halfback in motion made a hard-running overthrow on
Frontside Three.

The quarterback, coming away from the line straight
back as on the trap play, flash-faked the football beneath the
fullback's raised elbow. We did not want the ball to touch the
fullback, but absolute necessity demanded that it go under
the elbow to freeze for just a moment the linebackers who we
hoped had been conditioned by our successful operation of
the trap. An occasional reminder to the ball handler to
squeeze the ball with both hands during this fake prevented
fumbles that might have occurred when the ball accidentally
bumped some part of the fullback as the two men passed
each other on the run.

The fullback started forward exactly as on the trap play
with near elbow chin-high and far hand palm up below the
belt buckle showing the nice big pocket the backfield men always presented their quarterback. The instant the quarterback took the ball away from him, the fullback clamped both
arms together as if he were lugging leather, pushed off his
third step for the trap hole, and, provided he was not tack-

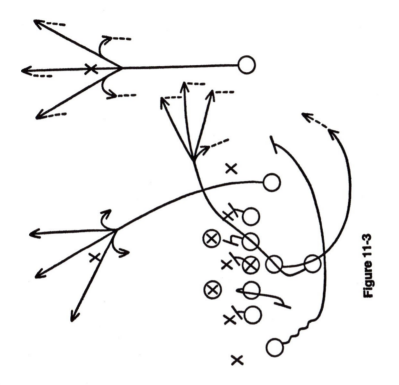

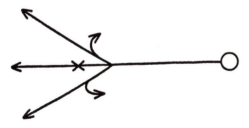

Figure 11-3

131

led, drove through the line on his way to the flat (Polecat Heaven) as a pass receiver.

The man in motion had no easy task in his overthrow on Frontside Three because this defender was too far removed from the trap hole to be much influenced by the fake. Still the halfback's job was to get the man, and get him good, for the quarterback wanted eight steps in which to deliver the ball.

The passer's number-one choice was the frontside end, who made a decision on his fifth step, took a few more steps to toss in what faking he wished to perform (our kids enjoyed making up their own fakes), and then set sail on his course. Before he had taken more than a couple of steps into the cut, the quarterback had to get the pass started on its way so that the receiver could enjoy whatever advantage he had picked up on his defender.

AUTOMATIC BLITZ

When Frontside Four lined up in the Blitz position, we were in trouble if we tried to go through with the eight-step Popcorn Pass; so, as on Gangster Pass Blitz and Cowboy Pass Blitz, the quarterback and the frontside end automatically teamed up for the Popcorn Pass Blitz (Figure 11-4). The end took his cue from the Blitz position of Frontside Four and on his third step cut inside at his 30 degree angle. The quarterback with the same cue took his customary two steps backward to get his fake made to the fullback, pushed toward the sideline, and flipped the Blitz Pass on his fourth step.

POPCORN SCREEN PASS

When Backside Three was consistently putting on a crash, the Popcorn Screen Pass took care of the ambitious fellow (Figure 11-5). On Popcorn Right, Screen Left, the left end stalked the defensive halfback on his side and threw a block into him the moment the man checked his backward

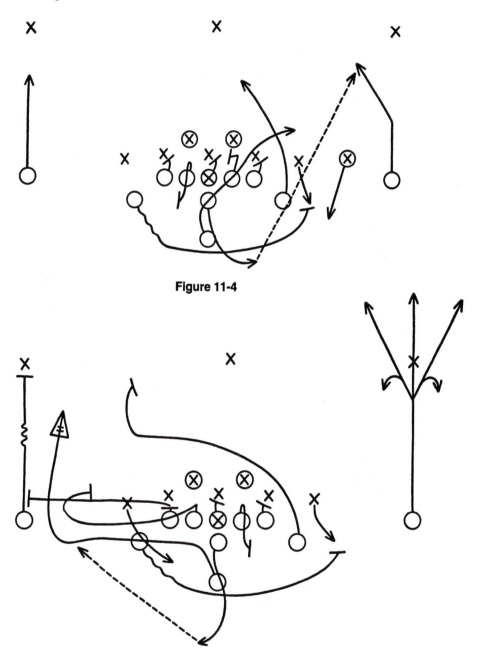

Figure 11-4

Figure 11-5

motion and started forward. The right end ran his toying operation against the defender on his side.

The left tackle jabbed a high hard shoulder (either) into Backside Two and headed for the sideline to block out on Backside Four should he escape from our left end. The left guard used the same operation on Backside One and followed the tackle toward the sideline until he heard the fullback yell, "Go!" just as the passer released the ball. This signal turned the guard downfield for the first opponent coming out from the inside. The other linemen blocked as on any pass play to their left. The left halfback ran hard for his usual overthrow on Frontside Three, while the right halfback cut shallow for the far side hook area from which he turned downfield on Backside Five as the ball was passed.

The fullback ran his trap course for two steps, showing the quarterback a big pocket for the football, and after his second step shoved off his right foot straight toward the sideline. As Backside Three rushed past him on the outside, he turned and looked for the pass over his left shoulder as he continued under control toward the sideline. Notice that our screen-pass receiver was *moving*—he was not dilly-dally-shilly-shallying around waiting for the football. All Run-and-Shoot people get into action.

The quarterback, making his trap fake to the fullback, completed three steps straight backward looking on his third step intently toward Frontside Four as if seeking a pass cue on the frontside and then turning suddenly to the backside ready to pass the ball on his sixth step to the fullback. If Backside Three tried to upset the dope bucket by not crashing, the quarterback took a few more steps to draw the crash. After that a scramble was on (Figure 11-6). However, there was seldom any need to scramble on the Popcorn Screen Pass—it enjoyed great success.

ANOTHER USE FOR THE SCREEN PASS

We made excellent use of the Popcorn Screen Pass in a situation different from against a crashing Backside Three.

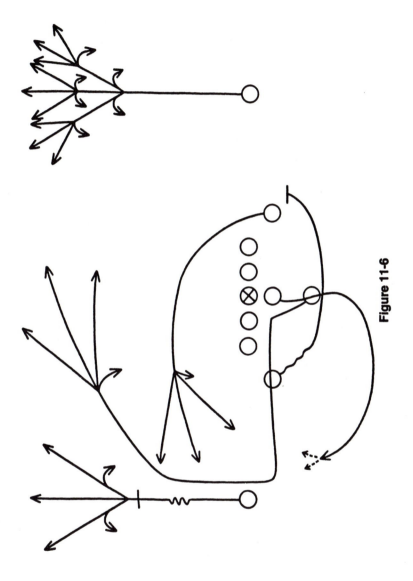

Figure 11-6

135

Sometimes the opponents used this man to go in motion with our halfback in motion to overload our frontside. One night against a team using these tactics, we hit the screen pass eight times in eight tries enabling our fullback, who had fewer chances to catch passes than any of our other receivers, to set a new school record for the number of passes caught in a single game (Figure 11-7).

POPCORN THROWBACK PASS

Although the Gangster with its longer motion and the Wagon Train with its fast frontside flow of men were our best series for throwback passes, still we gave each of the other series its own special throwback. We figured that any night we were going hog-wild to the frontside with a particular series that we should hit the backside with that same series; therefore, each series had its own throwback pass.

The Popcorn Throwback was identical to the one thrown from the Cowboy series except that we used Popcorn ball handling (Figure 11-8). The play worked better if the quarterback could get eight steps before delivering the ball to the backside. If he had to scramble, the pattern spread out exactly like the Cowboy Scramble.

POPCORN SERIES A GOOD ONE

The Popcorn series with its version of the T formation's greatest trap play gave our offense a much needed inside play up the middle. When this play was functioning well, it set up the Popcorn passes, which depended for their success on a well-executed fullback trap. The Popcorn was a fine series—it paid its own way.

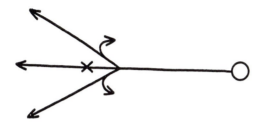

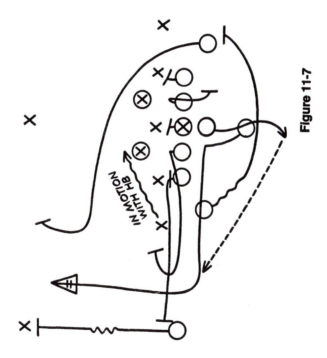

IN MOTION
WITH HB

Figure 11-7

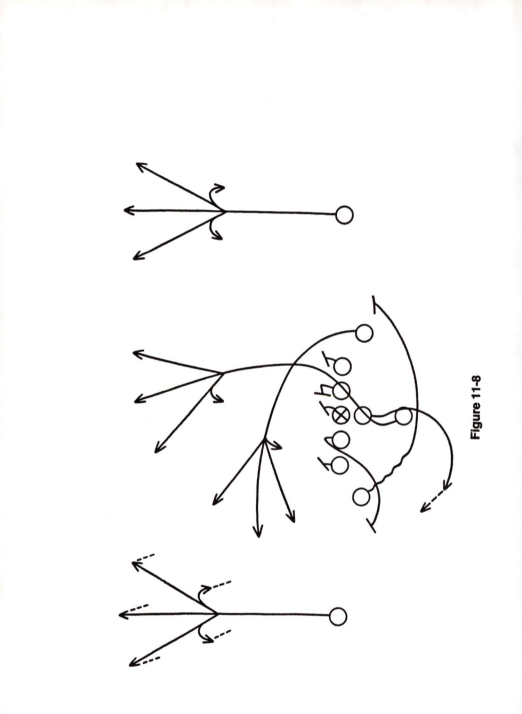

Figure 11-8

138

Chapter 12

Operation Mudcat

We completed our Run-and-Shoot offense with the addition of the Mudcat Series. We figured that on rainy nights when the field became a hog pen of mire and our Gangster was cornered and our Cowboy was grounded, we would have to roll east and west with the Wagon Train and north and south with the Popcorn and the Mudcat.

REASONS FOR THE MUDCAT

Although the rainiest nights we encountered during the four years did not stop the Gangster and the Cowboy—for they were never stopped—the Mudcat turned out to be a valuable asset against loose defenses that deployed their forces in accordance with two basic principles:

1. "Since they hurt you wide with their sweeps and their option plays, and since their passer must run wide to do his best work, we can frustrate these operations by ganging up on both corners, double-covering the flanks."

2. "Since their best inside play is the fullback trap up the middle, we can slow this operation by making our guards trap conscious."

Thus a four-man line became popular against us, a defense with both ends in Walkaway position and both cornermen in Hardnose (Figure 12–1).

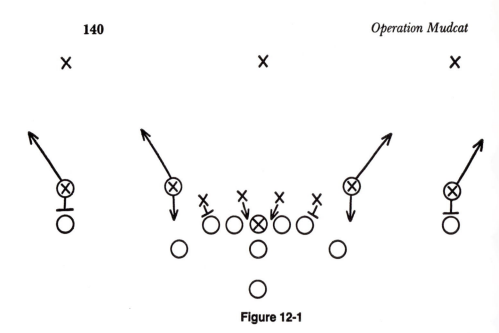

Figure 12-1

Let's try to work the Gangster Pass against this defense:

1. The quarterback orders his team to set at the line of scrimmage after calling Gangster Pass Right in the huddle.

2. There is no Automatic Pass to the backside end because of the head-on deep defender (Figure 12–2).

3. The Red-Dog Pass is in order because the inside linebacker is gone (Figure 12–3). This play looks great but we cannot work it fifty times a ball game.

4. The Blitz Pass is absolutely out (Figure 12–4) because Frontside Three is standing in the line of fire.

5. The Walkaway Pass is in a bind (Figure 12–5), for we cannot get a two-on-one situation because again Frontside Three muddies up the pond.

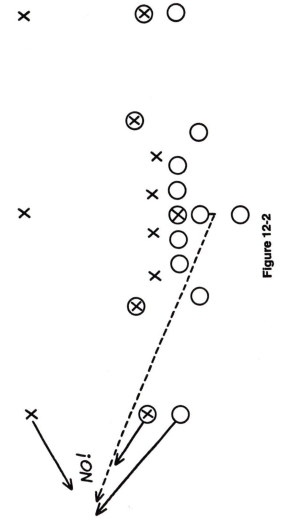

Figure 12-2

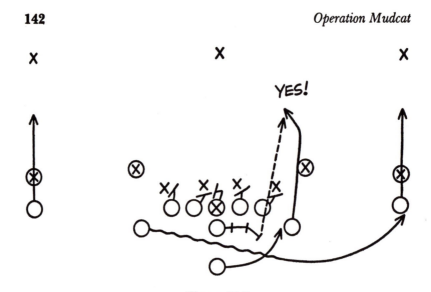

Figure 12-3

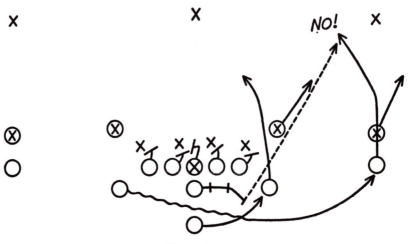

Figure 12-4

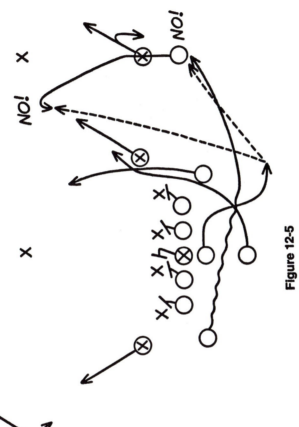

Figure 12-5

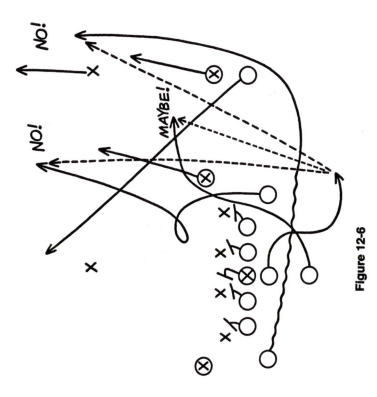

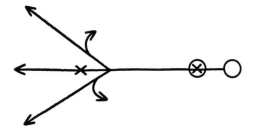

Figure 12-6

144

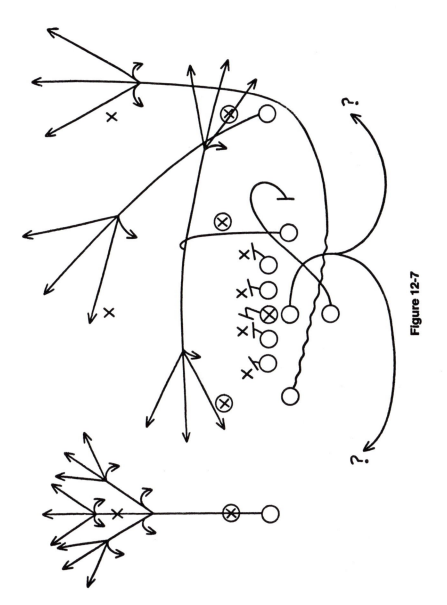

Figure 12-7

145

6. The Hardnose Pass is in much trouble (Figure 12–6) because there is just too much enemy color in the area.

7. Unless we have thrown Gangster Pass Red Dog, we very probably will go into a scramble (Figure 12–7). Just what will happen in a scramble is anybody's guess. If the seven defenders stay dropped off, certainly they should be able to cover a pass, causing the quarterback to gun his motor and lug leather. If the flank defenders come forward to stop the trigger man's run he probably will find a receiver somewhere to shoot at. However, we did not wish to scramble more than 10 percent of the time.

8. We need to rough them up a bit in the soft belly.

ENTER THE MUDCAT

Although the Cowboy did well against seven-man-dropped-off defenders with double-coverage on both our ends, and the Wagon Train rolled merrily on, and the Popcorn Trap outside the inside-conscious guards went well, still we wanted something extra special for any defense that double-covered our flankers. Our basic principle was this: they have to play us with at least three men deep; if they place two other men on our split ends, they will altogether have removed five men from close proximity to the football, leaving us with nine people to handle six (Figure 12–8). Any way they shuffle these close defenders, the thing still adds up nine to six in our favor. If we cannot beat them with these odds, we certainly are in a tough league—we should have stood in bed. So we called in the Mudcat.

MUDCAT SMASH

The Mudcat Smash enabled the fullback to hit straight ahead with power instead of having to veer behind the block

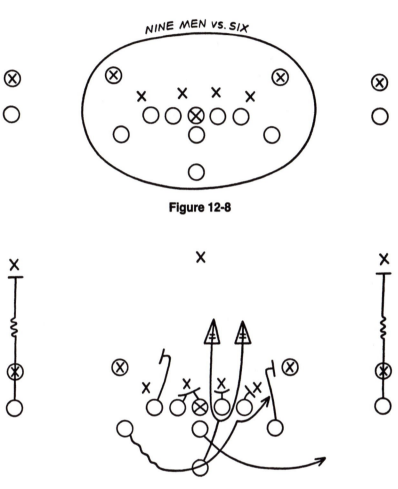

Figure 12-8

Figure 12-9

of the trapping guard as on the Pop Corn Trap (Figure 12-9). On Popcorn Smash Right the right tackle drove out on Frontside Two, while the right guard speared Frontside One right on the fellow's number with his forehead, taking him whichever way he chose to go. The center, if there was no Number Zero, helped his left guard with Backside One. The left tackle drove to the inside of Backside Two and turned back on the first man pursuing from the backside. The right halfback drove out on Frontside Three. The right end studied Frontside Five for five steps and threw an open field block on him the moment he checked his backward course and started forward. The left end maneuvered against Backside Five with a toying action, because we planned to throw from the Mudcat the same as from our other four formations.

The quarterback took a short step with his right foot straight backward and placed the ball upon the fullback's stomach under the latter's left elbow. At the instant of the hand-off the quarterback returned all his weight to his left foot and immediately stepped off again with his right foot 45 degrees away from the line of scrimmage, placing both his hands upon the faking left halfback's stomach as he drove by. Then the quarterback continued his run backward and outward with both hands upon his right hip while gazing intently at Frontside Four as if studying him for a pass cue. This was no stagnant quarterback. There had been no hesitation between his steps as he handled the ball—he had moved right foot, left foot, right foot with the same rhythm he used in all his controlled running.

The fullback at the snap signal sprang straight at the tail of his right guard, showed the quarterback a chin-high left elbow while placing his right hand palm upward below his belt buckle, and clamped the ball with both hands as he drove right or left of his guard, depending on which way Frontside One was being taken.

The left halfback away on short motion planted his right foot at the snap signal and drove straight for the tail of his right tackle, clamping both arms together the instant he felt the quarterback's faking hands upon his stomach. Then he veered to the right of his tackle in order to set up his teammate's block on Frontside Two.

MUDCAT DRIVE

If we could hurt the opposition just a little bit with the Mudcat Smash, then we were due for a piece of yardage with the Mudcat Drive (Figure 12–10).

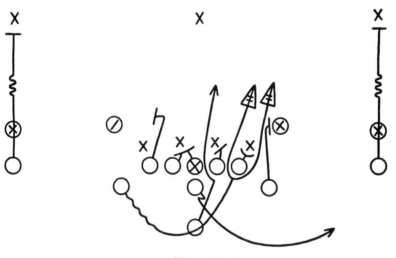

Figure 12-10

The blocking was the same as on the Smash except that the left guard drove in and the left tackle used the spear.

The ball handling was the same except that the quarterback flash-faked the ball to the fullback—placed it under his elbow and immediately jerked it back upon his own stomach as he shifted his weight back to his left foot—and gave it to the halfback as he stepped off again.

The fullback faking straight at his right guard clamped both arms the instant the ball disappeared from beneath his raised elbow and veered to the left of his guard to set up the block on Frontside One. The left halfback on his break toward the line studied his right tackle's block on Frontside Two and cut accordingly.

Early in its history the Mudcat Drive had a bad reputation—it was noted for its many fumbles. We cut down on much of this fumbling by making a couple of changes:

1. Where we had been riding the ball to the fullback, we put in the flash fake instead.
2. Where we had given the quarterback no alternative but to hand the ball to the halfback, we now permitted him to keep it—whenever he had a bad handle—and drive up behind the left halfback (Figure 12–11).

We liked this maneuver so well that we put it in as Mudcat Keep Right (or Left).

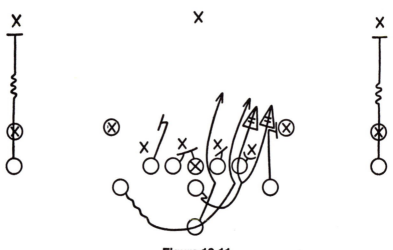

Figure 12-11

MUDCAT UP THE RIVER

Another play that cured our opponents of having a six-man front against us was the Mudcat-Up-the-River Play (Figure 12–12). The fullback, after the quarterback took the ball away from him, veered to the right of Frontside One to set

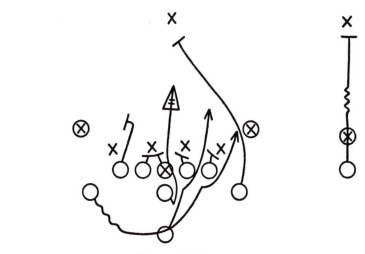

Figure 12-12

him up for the right guard's block. On this play the quarter-back went back to the original ride we had previously made on all Mudcat plays, because the ride to the fullback not only made the play look like the genuine Smash but it also helped pull the quarterback around and get him started on his course up the river. Another change was the right halfback's downfield block on the safety man.

MUDCAT JUMP

Although we certainly could have used Gangster Pass Red Dog against any defense that had no interior linebackers, still we wanted an equivalent when operating the Mudcat Series. We found it in the Mudcat Jump Pass (Figure 12–13).

The quarterback's backward step with his right foot was followed by a second step with his left foot bringing his feet together as he faked to the fullback. Then a jumping turn into the air off both feet brought his shoulders perpendicular to the flight of the ball. The pass was a simple wrist flip five yards straight ahead of the right halfback over his inside shoulder, old stuff and easy to do.

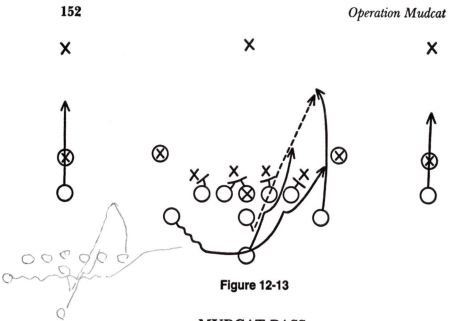

Figure 12-13

MUDCAT PASS

Our regular running pass from the series was called simply Mudcat Pass (Figure 12–14). It was a dandy. It was thrown against a shell-shocked safety man.

On Mudcat Pass Right the center against an even defense—with nobody over him—drove straight down the line of scrimmage for an overthrow block on Frontside One; against an odd defense he obviously would have taken the man over him. The right guard pulled as on Wagon Train East for an overthrow on Frontside Three. The blocking of the other linemen was normal.

The fullback, the instant the quarterback removed the ball from below his elbow, cut sharply on his third step behind the overthrow block of the center and drove, bent over and arms clasped, downfield looking intently at the safety man. The left halfback, with his arms similarly clamped also like a ball carrier, drove hard into anything hostile that appeared in his regular path.

The right halfback went for the inside position he always tried to get on Frontside Three during all Mudcat plays to his side, bumped him, and rushed into the frontside flat.

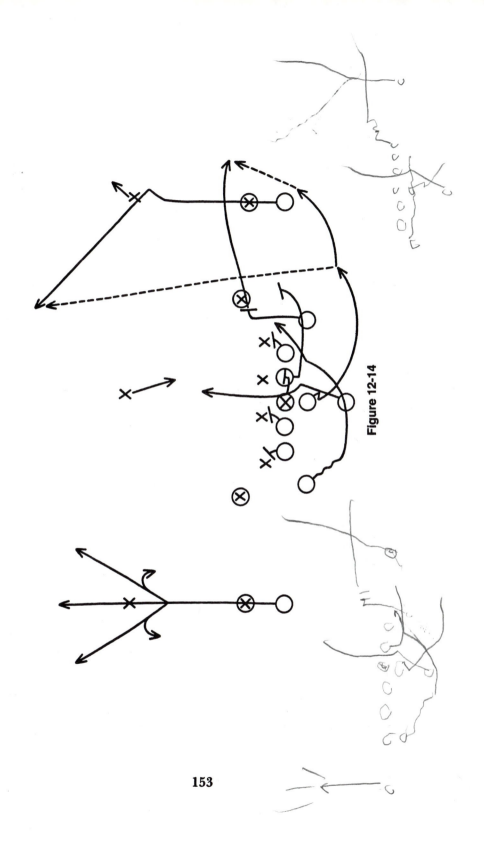

Figure 12-14

The quarterback after his two flash fakes, one to the fullback and the other to the left halfback, rolled out at a 45 degree angle and looked for his right end as his first choice.

For the first and only time in our Run-and-Shoot offense we assigned a specific cut to a deep receiver: the right end broke toward the defensive halfback under control as always, planted his right foot on his seventh step toward the flag on the goal line, and pushed off for the goal posts, looking for the pass over his inside shoulder. This specific cut was ordered with the idea in mind that we could now get behind the safety man. The pass had been held in reserve until we had hammered so much with the Smash and pounded so often with the Drive with an occasional Jump Pass mixed in, that we found the safety man coming up and making tackles close to the line of scrimmage. Now was the time for the long bomb arched high and aimed far.

We wanted the quarterback to turn the ball loose on his ninth step, for the right end would have taken only a couple of steps into his postward cut at that moment. The forward-backward-forward rocking of the quarterback as he made his two flash fakes at the beginning of the play counted as three steps (Figure 12–15).

Whenever the quarterback on his ninth step (ten going left) did not like what he saw deep, a scramble was in the offing except that again as on the Cowboy Pass it started with something specific, definite, solid, good: the quarterback turned downfield to draw Frontside Four forward so he could push a little pass to the right halfback in the flat or to lug leather himself if Frontside Four refused to leave his backed-off position (Figure 12–14).

MUDCAT THROWBACK

The throwback pass from the Mudcat Series was similar to those worked from the other series (Figure 12–16). Actually the only difference was the Mudcat ball handling.

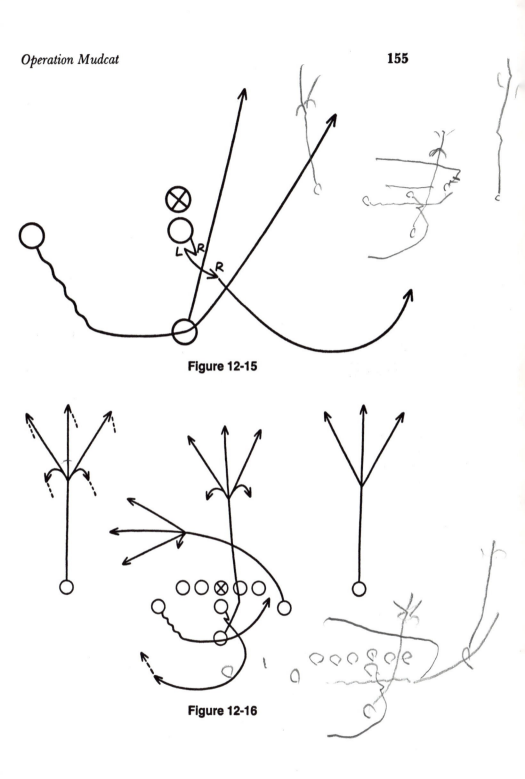

Figure 12-15

Figure 12-16

MUDCAT WELCOME

The Mudcat Series was a welcome addition to our Run-and-Shoot offense. It gave us inside strength against people who regarded ours solely as a wide-striking attack. It joined the Popcorn Trap in supplying north-south movement to our east-west operations. It gave us a long bomb down the middle against defenses that we could bend in the belly until the safety man started making tackles near the line of scrimmage. On rainy nights with the playing field a quagmire we often relied on Operation Mudcat.

Chapter 13

Picking the Personnel

While the Run-and Shoot Offense demands movement it does not necessarily require great speed, and it certainly puts no premium on size. The offense puts the emphasis where it belongs—on *skillful movement.* People will pay to see skillful performance.

The immediate job of any athletic coach is to teach physical skills to his players. If during the season he so motivates his young men that they carry on without his guidance in the off-season, that coach is bound for a successful career.

THE QUARTERBACK

The heart and soul of the offense is the quarterback. All our Run-and-Shoot quarterbacks made the all-state team, but they certainly did not look like all-state players when they first came in from junior high school. None of them was rated great as a passer by his junior high coach, though all were recommended as better than average ball handlers.

We selected from each incoming class the two boys who most nearly filled the following requirements:

1. He had a school history of being a good, solid citizen, quality stuff. Then if he developed sufficient skill to serve as our quarterback, he would be respected for what he was and for what he could do.

His teammates would follow him, his classmates would cheer for him, and the community would pay to see him perform, all so vitally necessary for a going operation.

2. His school record indicated he was interested in getting an education. Then he would consider football as a part of the educative process by which an individual develops himself to his fullest potential as a human being.

3. He was loose-jointed with a seeming knack for handling the ball, because ball-handling would become his middle name.

4. He could move with at least fair speed, for he certainly would have to do a lot of moving.

5. He came with an eagerness to play, because we wanted his motivation to reach the point where he would gather his receivers about him in the off-season. The summertime was the time when fair passers became good and good ones great.

THE SPLIT ENDS

The ends above all else had to catch the football. We wanted the ball to become a part of their anatomy once they touched it. They did not have to be big—they could be little, even skinny. We hoped they had speed, but we would not bench them as long as they could catch better than anybody else. The split-end position was no place for an awkward boy, for his chief operation was faking his defensive halfback and getting himself free for a pass. It was not neessary that he be a real hardnose, although he needed sufficient courage to make his downfield blocks on deep defenders. He had to be ambitious enough to heed the quarterback's call in the off-season, especially in the summertime, because summertime was "the time when fair receivers became good and good ones great."

THE FULLBACK

Number one, the fullback had to demonstrate a love of contact because the first thing we asked him to do was make a hard-driving overthrow on Gangster passes. Number two, he had to show a great desire to storm the castle, to crack the line, because the Cowboy, the Popcorn, and the Mudcat wanted him running hard to the inside. Number three, he had to show a willingness to become a great faker whose fakes looked like the real thing, the genuine article, because half his blast through the line would be without the football to set up the outside maneuvers, runs or passes, of the Cowboy and the Popcorn and the Mudcat. If he also had some speed, we would often send him wide on the Gangster Run. The Run-and-Shoot fullback was a good football player.

THE HALFBACKS

The first requirement of the halfbacks was ball-carrying ability. They needed speed, because an effective Wagon Train Sweep struck suddenly for distance and set up a great scoring weapon in the quarterback's fake to the halfback followed by a throwback to the backside. Secondly, a halfback had to be a catcher of footballs, second only to the ends in this respect, though most of his receiving was of a shorter nature with less maneuvering. Then, too, he needed to make a great effort in his own use of the fullback's hard-running overthrow block when a Cowboy Pass had been called. Also very important was his wide faking toward the sideline at top speed for ten yards as he glared at the corner man. Halfbacks arrived in assorted sizes, but the good ones came to play.

THE CENTER

The center was a character kid, a dedicated lad devoted to his quarterback, one of the trigger man's best friends, who was happy to pair up with him in all off-season ball-handling congregations. He was humbly content to squat and snap the ball hours on end. He did not need great ability—he needed desire, dedication, and devotion, because his vital spot in the line-up was so often unheralded by those who sat in the stands. Many of our centers were strong, silent, solid people whom you would be happy to have your daughter marry.

THE GUARDS AND THE TACKLES

In a ball-displaying offense in which everybody gets to play with the football except the guards and the tackles, how do you motivate these sturdy fellows who blaze the way for your offense to move? We appealed to their pride: "We selected you because we consider you the toughest kids on the squad, the toughest kids in this community. We think you boys would be willing to beat a grizzly bear to death with a ball bat if you had to. We believe you will turn out to be the toughest kids in all the communities on our schedule before the season is over—and that will make us a great ball club. Just how soon we become a great ball club depends on just how fast you fellows come along. You are the real power behind the Run-and-Shoot offense."

Chapter 14

The Daily Practice Plan

During the dog days of August, which was what we called the early days of football practice before school started, we used to practice for two hours twice a day, starting at eight o'clock in the morning and four o'clock in the afternoon. But when we saw all the ball handling, the passing and the catching, required by the new Run-and Shoot offense, we split the four hours of practice time into three daily sessions instead of two.

BALL-HANDLING DRILL

The eight-o'clock and the four-o'clock sessions were cut to an hour and a half each. Sandwiched between these two regular work sessions was a one-hour ball-handling practice for only the ball handlers, everybody except the guards and the tackles. It started at one o'clock sharp.

Dressed only in shorts and shoes, three groups of ball handlers lined up and went through the five series of plays like a basketball team running through its bunny-shot drill (Figure 14–1). As soon as the first group ran a play, the second bunch stepped up and ran theirs, and then the third. By that time the first group was back, ready to go again. There was no walking back to set up for another play—they jogged back. There was no standing, no waiting—it was constant movement, continuous motion. Any coach who wished to correct a boy after a play went forth to meet him and jogged

FIRST
TEAM

RUN PLAY

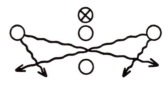

SECOND
TEAM

JOG UP

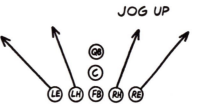

THIRD
TEAM

JOG UP

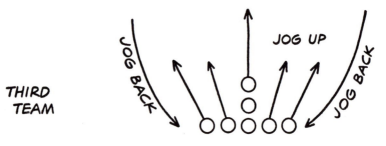

Figure 14-1

back with him. He made his correction in conversational tones. There was no standing around by raving coaches shouting their coaching points with a lordly look down the long skinny snout. The coaching staff flowed with the stream of motion. It was human bodies moving in accord with a moving ball. It was fun. It was Run-and-Shoot.

Exactly at the stroke of two, one hour later, the whistle blew, and the action stopped. The players went back into the cool confines of the stadium and lay down upon mats and relaxed for one hour, slept if they could. At three o'clock they started getting taped for the regular four o'clock practice.

We told our guards and tackles that since they were the hardest workers on the squad with the toughest work to do, they need not report for the one o'clock sessions—they could stay home and rest. The amazing thing was that half these fellows came back at one o'clock and asked permission to play with a football on another field—it was their only chance to get their hands on the ball.

THREE-A-DAY SESSIONS ACCEPTED

We thought at first that three practices a day would bring down a storm of protests from the parents. These were the hottest days of the year. Some of the local medicine men had long looked askance at our early head-knocking activities during the double sessions of our old possession days. However, there was no squawking from the parents, no desist orders from the doctors. Everybody was happy with Run-and-Shoot football.

PRE-PRACTICE WARM-UP

At the start of a regular practice session, the players came from their short inside meetings with their coaches (the best place to coach is on the field) and jogged twice around the field to get the circulation going. Then the whistle blew and they assembled for five minutes of calisthenics. We carry no brief for calisthenics except that they are a nice discipline, when led by the team captain, for warming-up before a ball game.

Exactly one and a half hours after the whistle, they would head for the showers. We found that keeping them even five minutes overtime was a good way to start wrecking morale. There were times in the rugged past when we kept them as much as an hour overtime to punish them for a bad practice. The years taught us that you can do anything in the world to a boy so long as he thinks that what you are doing is good for him and the team. But let him get the idea you are punishing him and he immediately shrivels up and becomes progressively worse as the overtime wears on. Anything negative gnaws away at morale. Our Run-and-Shoot philosophy was one hundred percent positive.

After the calisthenics the squad paired off for two form tackles with each shoulder and a couple of overthrow blocks each way. Then there was a 40-yard dash by position with the winner and the runner-up in each group dropping out while the others ran again, not to *punish the losers,* but to *reward the winners.*

GROUP WORK OF THE LINEMEN

Formal practice now began. The guards and the tackles and half the centers went with their coaches for drills on the sled, to be followed by work for one hour on the fundamentals they would use in a game, offensively and defensively. Some players were solely offensive; others, defensive; a few, both. Just how much time they spent on a fundamental was determined by a formula we got from Woody Hayes:

1. The percent of time they would use it in a game.
2. Its importance to the play.
3. Its degree of difficulty.
4. The skill with which our linemen could perform it.

If we found in analyzing the skills required by our offense (and defense) that some were used much more often than others, we gave those things more time. If some skills were used less but were vitally important, they still got a lot of time. Complex tasks that could not be simplified received plenty of time. Those things which our linemen did easily did not receive as much attention, while those things that caused them particular trouble got special treatment.

GROUP WORK OF THE BALL HANDLERS

Meanwhile the ball handlers, including the other half of the centers, gathered an hour for their drills against a skeleton defense. Time allotments for the five offensive series were as follows:

Gangster	20 minutes
Cowboy	15 minutes
Wagon Train	8 minutes
Popcorn	8 minutes
Mudcat	8 minutes
Total	59 minutes

We started first by working all Gangster plays with the left halfback in motion and went for ten minutes against a defense consisting of all frontside defenders except Frontside Two since we had no tackle to handle him (Figure 14–2).

We asked Frontside One to be a linebacker, for we had no guard to take him if he played on the line. The centers took turns playing Number Zero and gave each other token resistance so that they could get the feel and the fit of their blocks.

Frontside Three varied his charge from an inside slant to an outside crash to a straight charge and sometimes he wrestled with the right halfback to keep him from getting out. Frontside Four lined up in any of his three positions: Blitz, Walkaway, or Hardnose. Each of the other defensive men made an honest effort to intercept the football but used a shoulder bump or a two-handed push instead of a real tackle when passes were completed or a running play developed. Thus these defenders were getting work on pass coverage and pursuit even though we restricted their actual

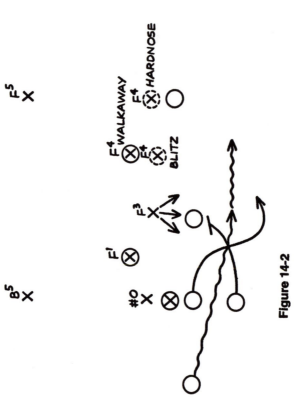

Figure 14-2

tackling. After ten minutes the drill was reversed for work on all Gangster plays starting with the right halfback in motion.

Then fifteen minutes were spent on Cowboy plays right and left against exactly the same defensive set-up (Figure 14–3). The Wagon Train followed with eight minutes devoted to its ramifications (Figure 14–4).

For the Wagon Train we removed Frontside One from the defensive group since we had no guard to handle him. The Popcorn Series also went its eight minutes without involving Frontside One for the same reason (Figure 14–5). We concluded the ball handlers' group work with eight minutes devoted to the Mudcat, again with no Frontside One (Figure 14–6). Thus we spent one hour of our regular practice, two thirds of the total time, on these basic maneuvers, for these things were the Run-and-Shoot offense.

TEAM WORK

The last half hour of practice was spent with the team working as a unit full blast—game conditions—against a sophomore defense. We did not then, but we certainly would now, have the defensive unit on another part of the field working its defense against a sophomore offense. We opposed ourselves with sophomores in order that we could practice with success rather than get frustrated with failure. Remember that Run-and-Shoot football requires an attitude one hundred percent positive. We replaced the sophomores often so that they would not get gun-shy from the shelling. Incidentally, a number of sophomores made our defensive team each year because of their fine work in these scrimmages.

When shower time came at the end of an hour and a half, shower time it was—the Run-and-Shooters departed from the field on the run. Forecast for tomorrow: same time, same station, same program, except that some boys may move up because of their fine work today!

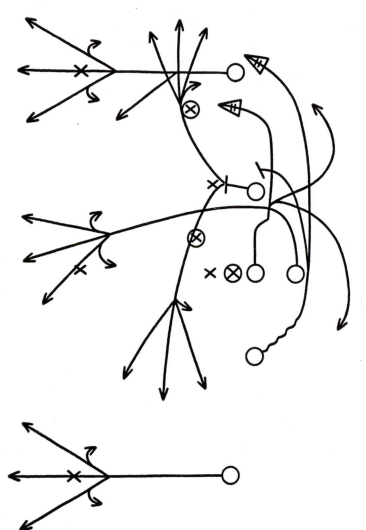

Figure 14-3

168

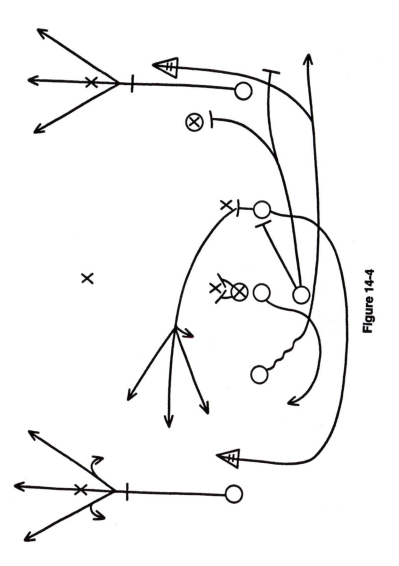

Figure 14-4

169

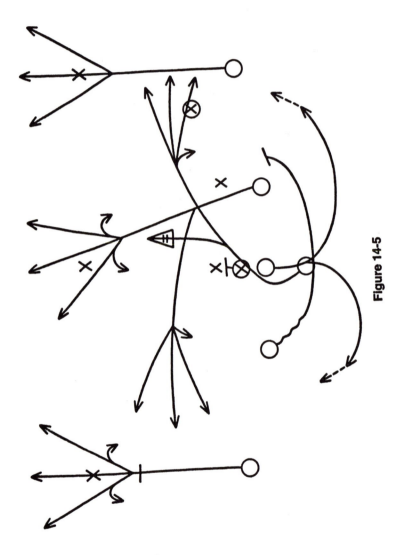

Figure 14-5

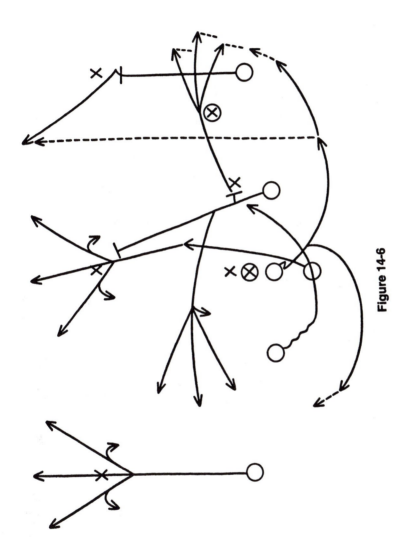

Figure 14-6

171

Chapter 15

What Makes Sammy Run-And-Shoot

GREAT PASSERS ARE MADE

"I would use a pass offense if I had a quarterback with natural passing ability."

Coach, did you ever make that statement? I did, many years ago. But I will never make it again. A thing called the *Lonesome Polecat* taught me that even though natural ability means ability furnished by nature, still, nature takes care of her own. If you come *asking* and *seeking* and *knocking*, you shall *find*. When any person with a great need puts a demand on nature, she comes through for him! Ask, seek, knock, and find. Thanks, Lonesome Polecat, for reminding me of a great lesson learned long ago.

LUCASVILLE, U.S.A.

I know of a town that took 33 years to win the state championship in basketball. Then those people became so enthusiastic over that championship that basketball goals sprang up all over town on every other garage, and that community went on to six more championships in the next twelve years. The athletes at first were just average American youngsters with average ability but they hit 46 percent of their shots game after game and year after year in an era when 35 percent usually won the ball game. They put a demand on nature by blazing away at those hoops, indoors and out, all year long, year in and year out, and nature came through for them by bringing them those six additional championships. During the last six of those twelve years a five-foot-seven-inch junior high youngster, whose father was not even six feet tall and whose mother was just average size, became so motivated by the city-wide demand that the high school win the state championship that he suddenly blossomed forth to six feet-eight inches in height and led his team to 76 straight victories and a couple of championships all by himself. His name was Jerry Lucas. *Put a demand on nature and she will see you through.*

PASSER WANTED

If you need a good passer for your football offense, you will get one. If you do not give the forward pass a chance in your offense, you do not need a passer, good or bad. If you are waiting for a great passer to come along before you put in your pass offense, then, coach, let's face it: you are a dreamer waiting for good luck to come your way. The man who sits dreaming of the day Santa Claus will come down the chimney and hand him a great passer ready-made may succeed someday, but his success will be accidental.

Pick out your young would-be quarterback, and let him know you expect him to be a great passer. Paint a clear vivid picture of your need in his mind. Brand it on his brain. Drive it into his heart. It will become an intense, burning, desire. It will grow into a gnawing need. Nature will answer the call, and you will have your passing quarterback with natural ability.

PASSER OBTAINED

I have coached eight all-state quarterbacks. One of them weighed 230 pounds, but another only 145. One could run the 100-yard dash in ten flat, while another took almost twelve seconds to do it. Two of them were honor students, but another flunked out of college. As passers none of them came in above average but all of them went out great. Natural ability? Yes, ability furnished by nature after those young men had thrown thousand of passes in the off-season because their coach expected them to be great tossing the football. Nature takes care of her own.

FOOTBALL TO THE FRONT

American football has become the great American Game. Upon the television screen in living rooms across the land have come weekend displays of the extravaganza that is football. The pro people deserve the credit, but the colleges and the high schools are following suit as they open their attack and display the football.

Youngsters fresh from the cradle have been popping their eyes at that romantic fellow known as Mr. Quarterback. No longer is it Mr. Railroad Engineer or Fire Chief or Indian Fighter or Band Leader, but Mr. Quarterback. Youngsters who used to gather themselves together ill-equipped and unsupervised on the sandlots to jostle each other over a toy football now cavort fully equipped on organized teams carefully supervised and coached by interested adults who know their business. People used to say a great baseball player grew up with a baseball glove sticking from his hip pocket. Today's youngster is growing up with a football on his lap. And football passers, with *natural ability*, are beginning more and more to arrive at the high school playing fields all about the country.

"I would use a pass offense if I had a quarterback with natural passing ability."

Coach, he is here.

POINTERS FOR THE QUARTERBACK COACH

Fathers, uncles, brothers, and other interested adults who today coach the Little Leagues on the gridiron have the greatest chance of teaching young quarterbacks the science of passing a football. Junior high coaches are next in line. High school mentors have the final opportunity. The boy coming to college is either a passer or he is not—he will change very little, although the college coach can polish him a bit. The pro coach gets the lad a trifle late to teach him anything about the actual passing of the ball, but he will give the boy plenty of opportunity to pass with cleverly contrived methods of getting his work done. The pro coaches eventually will reach the ultimate when they add the Run-and-Shoot triggerman firing on the move.

STUDYING THE FORWARD PASSER WITH MOVIES

A movie analysis of forward passers showed that a right-handed passer on the run started the ball back toward his ear the instant his left foot hit the ground. He began the snap forward the moment his right foot hit. In between were the basic techniques of any good passer, running or set.

1. The lean of the body downfield toward the target.
2. The pointing of the elbow away from the target.
3. The throwing of the elbow toward the target with the ball flying out as if hurled from a catapult.
4. The downward thrust of the fingers toward the ground as the ball was released.

We found an important difference between a running pass and one thrown from set. On a running pass the movement of the ball backward to a point behind the passer's head and then forward again to the point of release was lightning fast—so fast in fact that it took a slow-motion camera to record the action. We noticed that the pass stroke from a set position was longer and slower.

One day in practice we put our secondary defenders in a zone defense (our favorite) and ordered them to move with the passer's arm to the spot where the passer was looking. They did their best to carry out orders.

"But, Coach," they cried, "the pass was on its way before we saw his arm move!"

So we chalked up a big plus for the running pass.

RUNNING LEFT TO PASS

All of our Run-and-Shoot quarterbacks were as adept running to the left to pass as they were running to the right. In fact a couple of them preferred running to the left, which seemed surprising . . . until we studied the pictures. We saw that when running to the right they started their lean toward the target on the left foot, causing the right foot to cross over the left and plant itself downfield toward the target as the ball was snapped forward. But when running to the left, instead of making a crossover step, the right foot pulled away from the left on the step downfield. This open step seemed more natural than the crossover.

Also the right shoulder, which had to be forced back into a cocked position before making a running pass to the left, seemed to spring forward again of its own accord. It appeared that less effort was required to release a pass while running left.

Our final conclusion was that right-handed passing while running left is every bit as practical as that to the right.

PRO QUARTERBACK ON THE RUN

Have you ever seen a fine pro quarterback drop back into a pocket, start his pass motion forward, and then suddenly check the action with his other hand because of tight coverage or a breakdown in timing or protection? What did he do then? That splendid athlete suddenly went mobile: He scampered right or he scampered left, and then he arched the ball high up and far off into the Promised Land to a teammate cavorting there free and unencumbered. And the fans went hog-wild!

Motion! Emotion! Commotion! I know a sure way to keep those fans in a constant state of frenzy: Give them Run-and-Shoot football all the time.

DEVELOPING THE RUN-AND-SHOOT QUARTERBACK

Here, young man, is the way to do it:

1. Hold the football with both hands in front of your chest. Grip the ball gently. Don't squeeze it. If you squeeze, the muscles in your arm will tense up and you will have a rigid passing arm that cannot possibly snap off a running pass. Hold the ball lightly and feel the loose, rubbery muscles stretching from your hands to your shoulders. Feather that touch all the way through the passing action.

2. Now stand with your left side toward a stationary target ten yards away (Figure 15-1). This target can be your dad or your brother or a buddy or an old blanket hanging on the clothes line.

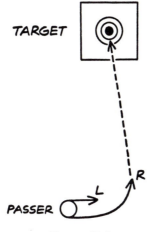

Figure 15-1

3. Step off with your left foot. As that foot hits the ground do two things simultaneously: Lean toward the target and bring the ball back behind your right ear.

4. Follow with your right foot. Because you have been leaning toward the target, your right foot will just naturally cross over your left and you will find yourself stepping downfield with that right foot. Good.

5. The instant your right foot hits the ground on this downfield step, snap the ball toward the target. If you have kept a light grip on the ball, the ball will fly out with very little effort.

After a while turn your right side toward the target and learn to pass going to the left (Figure 15-2). Again step off with your left foot and lean toward the target as that left foot strikes the ground. Notice that your right foot now, instead of crossing over left, open-steps downfield right. The ball starts back at the end of that first step as before and it starts forward at the end of the second step. However, there was one important difference in the action: the right shoulder had to be rolled backward about 45 degrees in order to cock the arm for the throw. This cocking of the arm sends the ball flying out with ease. You will find that throwing on the run to the left is just as easy as the other—if you roll the shoulder back and cock the arm.

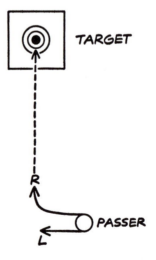

Figure 15-2

After you get pretty good at taking two steps and passing, you are ready to start jogging a few steps before throwing. Eventually you will be able to run under control any number of steps and snap the ball 40 yards downfield in the beautiful manner of the Run-and-Shoot quarterback. Actually you will seldom need to make a pass that long—most of your passes will be much shorter.

If you find yourself enjoying this work so much that you get out and throw passes by the hour, there may come a time when the high school coach will want you to quarterback his team. There may even come a day when some college coach will offer you a scholarship to come to his school. Then all your work will have been rewarded. Young man, good luck.

Chapter 16

Today's Coach Is an Educator

"Coach, we're hiring you first and foremost as a teacher. Among your duties we expect you to coach kids, to build boys, to mold men. We want these youngsters brought up the American way, which is a competitive way and a winning way. Winning is positive. Losing is negative. Let's be positive!"

A VIEWPOINT WELL TAKEN

The first statement in the above quotation is universal and is heard by every young coach as he sits in interview with those who hire. I heard it. You heard it. Others will hear it. The remainder of the quote may be implied. Sometimes it is implied gently. Yet it is there—it permeates the very atmosphere of the interview room. Sometimes it is implied forcefully, so much so that it ceases to be subtle.

The whole quotation wraps things up nicely in a viewpoint that is well taken. The spokesman speaks for a whole community whose pliable youth will be standing around you, looking up to you, ready to become you, during the years just ahead. The young people do not know what they want, but the grownups do—they want a winner. If they did not want a winner, they would not be worth working for. You would not like the job. It would not be thrilling, exciting, challenging. If they want a winner and you do not give it to them reasonably

180

soon, you will not like those people, nor will they like you. You might not even like yourself.

It certainly requires no great genius to know what a winner is: throw ten evenly matched teams together in a league in which they all play each other once in a nine-game schedule, and when the season is over hang the winner's tag on any team that has won five ball games. Crown the champion with a wreath of roses and stuff the runner-up with holiday turkey, but do not forget to shake hands with all the other winners too. Console the losers and give them a year or two to become winners. If you, Mr. School Board President, and you too, Mr. Chairman of the Athletic Council, do not recognize as a winner any team that wins one game more than it loses, you boys had better hurry yourselves off to the nearest preacher or priest or rabbi and get your souls whitewashed for you may be headed for hell fire and brimstone.

THE REAL CRITERION OF A GREAT COACH

The football coach, like the businessman, has only one problem: put out a winner. Ninety percent of America's coaches throw in the towel before completing 20 years in the profession. The same percentage of businessmen close their doors on a particular product long before that. The strong get stronger and the weak get weaker. Those who dominate the struggle all possess varying degrees of greatness.

You say to the successful man of business, "Push aside your million dollars and show me what real service you are rendering the people." You say to the successful coach, "Put away your record books and show me what the kids you coached, the boys you built, the men you molded, are doing today. What attitudes did you weld onto their natures that are helping them achieve their destinies as complete human beings?"

The businessman is great if he has made much money *and* contributed much service. The coach is great if he has won many games *and* molded many men. But the money and the victories alone do not prove the men great. The money and the victories are the working tools. What did they build with their tools?

VICTORY OVER DEFEAT

If you think you can mold a boy into a man without squeezing him pound by pound upon a framework of victory, just try losing all your games some season and see how much character you can teach that year, on the field or in the classroom or downtown or at home with your own kids. If you try to rationalize, you sound like a prating cry-baby. If you clam up and feel sorry for yourself, you look like a sick cow. You can either hold onto your hat as you toss it into the river or you can cuss a little—just a little—grit your teeth and clench your fists and analyze your mistakes and go back to work.

We lost four ball games and had only a tie to show for the first half of one season and one of my players sat on a river bank all night contemplating suicide. He was man enough to snap out of it—he came back next day, and we won the last five games, thanks to the Lonesome Polecat. We enjoyed that five-and-four season more than we enjoyed the nine seasons they proclaimed us great. We used each of those defeats to help us appreciate each of our victories, and we had an extra victory to boot around just for the pure exhilaration that victory over defeat brings.

Victory over defeat means one victory more than the number of defeats. We have done much better than that over the years, but I suspect that the greatest educational value comes, that more men are actually molded, in a victory-over-defeat season than in an all-victorious season. Winning them all is absolutely great if it represents a lot of sacrifice and a lot of all-out effort. But if it happens too often to the same people, they stop sacrificing, they slacken their efforts, and the thing is no longer educational.

SUPERINTENDENT CONFIRMED

A victory is not educational unless you can compare it with the defeat you were escaping. You lose sight of that defeat unless it occasionally catches up with you. You get into the habit of running straight on with your head back looking down your long skinny nose at the environment around you. An occasional defeat brings your head down and re-teaches an old lesson: A living organism must struggle for its place in the sun or it perishes.

Education is in process when you compare this week's victory with last week's defeat and realize what made the difference: better preparation, greater determination, more sacrifice, harder work.

"Coach, we're hiring you first and foremost as a teacher. Among your duties we expect you to coach kids, to build boys, to mold men. We want these youngsters brought up the American way, which is a competitive way, and a winning way. Winning is positive. Losing is negative. Let's be positive!"

The man was right.

Glossary

Backside—the side of the field opposite the direction of the half-back in motion

Blitz Pass—a quick pass designed to cope with an outside defender lined up on the line of scrimmage

Blitz Position—the position of a defensive end or an outside linebacker who lines up on the scrimmage line

Butcher-boy—an opponent whose assigned task is to tackle a faking quarterback with the purpose of removing him from the game

Cherry-pick—a football adaptation of the basketball screen block

Cherry-picker—a halfback whose job is to screen an interior linebacker to prevent his dropping back for pass protection

Clutch—the moments just before the end of the first half or the ball game

Collect-up—a maneuver applied to a passer when he runs to a stop by making his last couple steps quick and short

Corner Man—the outside defensive man on or near the line of scrimmage

Cowboy—term applied to a series of plays in which the quarter-back rides the ball to the fullback as the play develops

Crasher—a defensive end or corner man who rushes into the offensive backfield to upset the timing of the play

Cross-over—the crossing of the right foot over the left as a right-handed running passer throws while moving to his right

Daylight—an opening in the defensive line toward which a ball carrier is moving

Dead Polecat—a series of plays worked automatically from a peculiar spread formation in which the quarterback is unprotected eleven yards back of the ball

184

Drive Play—a halfback power play from the Mudcat Series in which the ball is faked first to the fullback

East—a play worked to the right

Eating the ball—the quarterback getting caught behind the line of scrimmage before he can get his pass away

Flat—the pass area on each side of the field close to the line of scrimmage

Frontside—the side of the field toward which the halfback goes in motion

Gangster—name applied to a series of plays in which a halfback goes in long motion before the ball is snapped from center. The series provides unlimited opportunities for "ganging up" on a pass defender

Hardnose Pass—a forward pass designed to cope with a defender lined up directly over a split end

Hardnose Position—position assumed by an end or corner man directly in front of an offensive split end

Heaven—the area near the sideline and close to the line of scrimmage toward which the halfback is going in motion

Hell—the opposite of Heaven

Leather Lugger—the ball carrier whose purpose is not to throw a pass but to get goalward as fast as he can go

Live Polecat—a series of plays in the Lonesome Polecat Offense, featuring a pass receiver moving behind a running screen of linemen

Lonesome Polecat—a peculiarly spread offense featuring a variety of plays with a scrambling quarterback

Meat-grinder—a power offense built principally on "getting there fustest with the mostest"

Mudcat Series—a group of maneuvers featuring straight ahead movements of the fullback and the halfbacks

On the ball—offensive players getting started at the snap of the ball instead of listening to verbal signals from the quarterback

Open-step—a step taken with the right foot downfield away from the left foot when a right-handed passer is running to his left

Overthrow—a special block used by the fullback on Gangster passes and by the halfbacks on Cowboy passes. The block is made while running at top speed

Penetrator—the first lineman or interior linebacker across the line of scrimmage in the path of the trap blocker during a trap play

Pocket Passer—a passer who drops back and sets up behind a wall of protecting linemen

Point of decision—the fifth step taken downfield by a deep pass receiver. At this point he must decide whether he will break left or right or straight ahead or stop

Popcorn—a series of plays featuring the greatest trap play in T formation football, the old Cleveland Browns' fullback trap

Red Dog—an interior linebacker who crashes into the offensive backfield at the snap of the ball

Red-Dog Pass—a pass designed to take advantage of an interior linebacker who crashes at the snap of the ball

Red, White, and Blue—patriotic names given to the three deep pass receiving areas. Red applies to the backside, White the middle, and Blue the frontside.

Run-and-Shoot—a football offense which defies the defense to analyze any of its plays as a run or a pass while the play is developing

Running Passer—a forward passer who delivers the football toward its target while he is running at top controlled speed

Scramble—a pass play whose timing has been upset by late receivers, poor protection, or indecision of the passer

Smash—a play in the Mudcat Series in which the fullback drives full-tilt at his guard, veering right or left according to his guard's block

Soft Backside—the side away from the halfback in motion which drops off the defensive end

Spear—a block which has an offensive lineman ramming his forehead into a defensive man's numbers to stop his charge and take him whichever way he wants to go

Stagnant Quarterback—one who comes to a stop before passing or faking a hand-off or making the hand-off. The Run-and-Shoot offense berates such tactics as artistically inept and labels them wormwood to sound football

Throwback—a forward pass made to a lonely backside end who calls his pass cut in the huddle after having studied his defender on previous plays

Unwelcome Stranger—a sixth defensive man who shows up on the frontside during the performance of a play, usually one from the Gangster Series with its longer motion

Up the River—a delayed quarterback sneak from the Mudcat Series

Victory-over-defeat—a football season in which a team has won one game more than it has lost. Such seasons are deemed winning seasons by all fair-minded people

Wagon Train—a series of plays featuring pulling guards and wide running halfbacks

Walkaway Pass—a forward pass designed to put a Walkaway defender in a bind in which he is wrong whatever move he makes

Walkaway Position—the position taken by a defensive end or corner man who drops a few yards off the line of scrimmage

INDEX